The Martha's Vineyard Cookbook

September 25, 2025

A Taste of Martha's Vineyard Comes to Boston!

Happy cooking!
♡Julia

Julia Blanter

The
Martha's Vineyard
Cookbook

100 Recipes from the Island's Restaurants,
Farmers, Fishermen & Food Artisans

Julia Blanter

FOREWORD BY JULI VANDERHOOP
PHOTOGRAPHY BY JOCELYN FILLEY

RIZZOLI
NEW YORK

New York · Paris · London · Milan

Contents

THE MARTHA'S VINEYARD COOKBOOK

Foreword

JULI VANDERHOOP

I am the youngest in my family and the only girl, with five older brothers. Most of our childhood summers were spent outside, roaming the hills and beaches as far as our legs would carry us. Back then we set off for the day with just the clothes on our backs— no sunblock, water bottles, lunch coolers, or even towels. Nonetheless, the freedom of those summers created the character that has shaped my life.

Following my brothers, who were five to fifteen years older than I, was no easy task, especially when we found ourselves across town after six hours of playing in the sun without water or a formal lunch. The trip back might have been much worse if my elders had not taught me many things about the lands around me. I would wander slowly each day, stopping at every stream and berry bush in order to build the energy needed to find my way home prior to six p.m., when I was due back. Many people think you need a degree to understand the environment around you, but growing up in a Wampanoag settlement in Aquinnah, we depended on that knowledge of our lands. This is a cornerstone of all Native American cultures.

When we gather to feast, some of the feast is reserved for the creator as thanks for the gift of the foods that we harvest. Many of our Tribe have left the island for better economies, but my family has stayed, continuing to work on every line cast in the community, from gathering, fishing, and hunting to working traditional wampum beads and even in politics. What we know about tending both the land and the sea is that each deserves our utmost respect in order to truly understand them. Watching the land change and communing on the lands together is a way of life for Wampanoag people on Martha's Vineyard. Our culture and livelihood have had to adapt to climate change, invasive species, toxins in our watersheds, and other challenges. Today we understand that with an outlook toward preservation, these lands, many held by Indigenous peoples, hold the keys to helping all of us understand the way the earth has worked for centuries.

My Orange Peel Bakery is located on Black Brook. This property has been gifted down to people in my family for decades. Often when I am working at the bakery, someone in my family will stop by bringing nettles, berries, or even seafood that they have foraged or gathered that day. Being a recipient of these offerings is part of the neighborly way that we have been taught to take care of one another, and each of these generous gestures warms my heart, reminding me why I am here.

The centerpiece of the bakery is a Le Panyol wood-fired oven that is ten feet in diameter and covered in fieldstone, just like the roadside stone walls built by Wampanoag people that have been here for centuries. I built it to look like it had been here forever. My father, Luther Madison, then the seated tribal Medicine Man, explained to me that the connection between the deep springs that run through our land here at Black Brook and the smoke from the fire within the oven would allow my ancestral spirits to remain close. Often, I look and listen for signs that the spirits are here to guide me, and there have been many along this journey. I believe that I am here with a purpose and that is to carry on our stories, many of which I tell or meditate into the food created in this oven. Working with the foods of my ancestors connects me to my people and tells the story of what helped us continue to stay on the land. This is an honor. In this book you will discover many recipes using native ingredients and it is an invitation to join us and break bread together. When we welcome new and old visitors to Martha's Vineyard, I share these stories, and I always hope they feel the respect and reverence we have for our island home. It is a magical place.

Introduction

There are many places that swell with the seasons, but few where visitors return year after year, decade after decade. What makes Martha's Vineyard so enticing? Is it the summertime charm of golden fried clams after a lazy, sun-kissed day on the beach? The nostalgia of lobster dinners under the tangerine glow of a Menemsha sunset, melted butter dripping down your chin? Or the freedom from schedules the moment you step aboard the ferry and realize that island time is just a hot dog or cold beer away? Is it your family's home that beckons, a gathering ground for annual rituals like trips to Morning Glory Farm for the freshest corn and strawberries and biking to Edgartown for ice cream and an afternoon porch session with a sundowner before a neighborhood clambake?

Even in fall and winter, when the island turns from green to gold to grayscale, punctuated by poinsettias and the bokeh of holiday lights, those who stick around are rewarded with the gifts of island life. The farms offer plenty of treasures: from squeaky fresh kale and tie-dyed radicchio to accompany a North Tabor Farm roast chicken to warm loaves and pastries that gratify the early-birders who dash to The Grey Barn bakery counter. Snowed-in days are the perfect excuse to steam up the windows with a pot of lamb stew or fish soup. You don't want winter to break, but then it does, and overnight the light changes and winter is in the rearview mirror. Daffodils herald the season; garden prep is in full swing. Grumbles about traffic and ferry reservations and talk of which restaurants will or won't return replace the quiet hum. The waters of Vineyard Sound always sparkle, but there is a flirtiness to the way the spring sun staccatos off the waves. Suddenly, you can't park anywhere, but you've snagged a fish sandwich by the water and all is good.

Martha's Vineyard is an island of 22,000 year-round residents, blooming to 200,000 in the summertime. Much of the mystique derives from its famous guests. As the seasonal retreat for former and standing presidents and the glitterati, the island has beckoned with its casual elegance and natural beauty for over one hundred years. Martin Luther King Jr., Jesse Jackson, and other civil rights leaders found refuge in Oak Bluffs. Carly Simon welcomed musicians from all over the world at her airport hang, Hot Tin Roof. Steven Spielberg chose the Vineyard to film a certain summer blockbuster—or was that Amity Island? There may not be any traffic lights, and the honor-box system is still delightfully present, but it's a world-class destination with undeniable draw. Museums and festivals spanning music, comedy, literature, and film nourish throughout the seasons, with a crescendo of events in August when actors, artists, and authors jet in for screenings, readings, performances, and general conviviality. Islanders don't tend to care much about star power—we're just happy to be here.

It surprises many that this is a real place with real people who eat, sleep, work, raise families, and spend their entire lives here. Yes, there are schools, supermarkets, and a hospital. No, there aren't fast food chains, minus a sole Dairy Queen—and this is something islanders have been proud of ever since McDonald's attempted to set up shop in 1979. The community is small but mighty, and social activism runs deep.

But it is important not to idealize. This is Wampanoag land, where People of the First Light have lived communally with tribal traditions and values for over twelve thousand years. A population of at least three thousand greeted the first European settlers in the 1600s, only to be brutally reduced in population to nine hundred members. Approximately three hundred Wampanoag people from the Tribes of Chappaquiddick and of Aquinnah live on their ancestral land today.

The Wampanoag name for the island, Noepe—dry land, or land amid the streams—seems more fitting than the name it was given by the English colonialist Bartholemew Gosnold in 1602 for his daughter (or mother-in-law, there's no definitive answer) in tribute to the agricultural vines running throughout the island. Fresh off the ferry, first-time visitors ask where the wineries are (only to discover there aren't any).

For African Americans, Martha's Vineyard, specifically Oak Bluffs (formerly known as Cottage City), became and remains a salt-air-infused respite from the contrarieties of the mainland. The island, once part of the underground railroad, was no stranger to the horrors of slavery. *The Green Book*, created by Victor Green in 1936 and inspired by similar guides for Jewish travelers, prompted its readers to "go further with less anxiety" and featured inns such as Shearer Cottage, opened in 1912 to cater to tourists who were not welcome elsewhere. Today, Inkwell Beach prevails as the beating heart of the community, where sunrise swims, yoga, and potlucks bring summer residents and visitors together.

Martha's Vineyard is not just lobster rolls and chowder. This is a melting pot with "washashores" (newcomers to the island) from just about everywhere, each bringing the unique flavors of their motherlands to the table. Portuguese is our second language, thanks to seafarers from the Azores who settled here in the late 1800s, and more recently Brazilians, who began to live and work hard on the island from the mid-1980s. Today they make up one-quarter of the year-round population. Your breakfast sandwich might just as likely come with linguiça as bacon. In addition, young Eastern Europeans arrive every summer to fill seasonal jobs through visa programs for foreign students. A small Caribbean population means that yucca, plantain, and okra sit alongside potatoes, corn, and beans in grocery aisles and market bushels. And for a snack, you can pick up a Jamaican patty or slice of wobbly flan as easily as fries and fudge.

Clambakes, that beloved summer ritual, are an important Wampanoag tradition. Succotash, the colorful vegetable dish adorning many summer tables, is another Indigenous recipe celebrating the season's bounty. Cranberry Day is observed in the town of Aquinnah every October. Today, Indigenous leaders such as Juli Vanderhoop follow in their ancestors' footsteps, revering food as medicine and the spirit of community. Pizza nights at her Orange Peel Bakery are an open-door affair, welcoming to all.

Farm-to-table was the way of life on the island before it became a marketing carrot to dangle in front of city diners. Beyond Edgartown, Oak Bluffs, and Vineyard Haven, the up-island towns of West Tisbury, Chilmark, and Aquinnah are largely rural and farmland. The first Agricultural Fair was held in 1858 and attended by 1,800 people—more than half the population at the time. The four-day fair continues to be the unmissable event of sweltering August, with tractor pulls, shearing contests, and blue ribbons on display—complete with the simple joys of factory-to-table corn dogs and cotton candy.

On the waterfront, the 124 miles of coastline and sixteen great ponds (those larger than ten acres in their natural state) are a rich source of food for the Wampanoag and all who have fished here since. Lobsters, oysters, clams, scallops, and dozens of varieties of fish reside in these pristine waters, and action to protect them is vital as overdevelopment from new homes and tourism threatens their sanctity.

Measures are also needed to ensure everyone in our community can continue calling this island home. The cost of living is 60 percent higher than the national average, with a desperate lack of affordable housing. The situation is broken; it's time to fix it.

This little nugget of an island twenty miles long, seven miles from "America," is home to over one hundred restaurants and cafés, fifty farms, five fish markets, four coffee roasters, two breweries, and one farmers market. While this is not an exhaustive collection of all the island has to offer, it is a snapshot of the talent and diversity that makes this a world-class culinary destination with something new and exciting to discover around every corner.

The *Martha's Vineyard Cookbook* is an invitation to hop, skip, and jump over to a magical island, one that may be new to you, on your bucket list, or deeply rooted in your family's DNA, and take a mouthwatering journey around its six towns. I hope this inspires delicious adventures and sustains you until your return.

With thanks to the Martha's Vineyard culinary community,

OPPOSITE (FROM TOP, LEFT TO RIGHT): Jo Douglas, Joy Younan, Naji Boustany; Stacy Thomas and Newton Waite, Zach Prifti, Korilee Connelly; Heather Pepper, Austin Racine and Maura Martin, Tyler Potter; Alex Said, Julia Tarka, Lexie Roth and Eva Faber; Brett Nevin, Ryan and Julia Smith, Kate Woods. **THIS PAGE:** Buddy Vanderhoop, Chrissy Kinsman, Anders, Jessica, and Greg Mason; Rachel and Jimmy Alvarado, Spring Sheldon, Brock Callen; Deva Randolph and Jessica Noe, Janelle and Stanley Larsen, Ann Khoan; Lily Walter, Chef Ting, Lydia Fischer

AQUINNAH

WAMPANOAG NAME: Âhqunah

Aquinnah is a sacred place.

The red clay of Moshup Beach glows against breathtaking sunsets. Dozens of stone towers dot the beach. The legend of Moshup is present. According to the Wampanoag, benevolent Moshup the Giant would catch whales to eat, flinging them against the cliffs and staining the clay blood red. From 1870, Aquinnah was known as Gay Head for the vibrant ochre colors of the cliffs. In 1997, a town vote changed its name to "land under the hill." It remains otherworldly, a place for reflection, restoration, and respect.

Visit the Aquinnah Cultural Center to explore Wampanoag history, art, and culture. And no drive to the westernmost tip of the island is complete without visiting the Gay Head Lighthouse, as it's still known, an icon with its own fascinating history. With erosion crumbling the land beneath it, the entire lighthouse was transplanted 134 feet inland to safety over two nail-biting days in 2015. No mean feat shifting a 400-ton brick structure!

our glorius
unsprayed
apple $ .50 ea

Todays Special
Buy 1 lb of
Any
Shrimp or more
Get a free cup
of
Chow or Bis.

CHILMARK

Chilmark is rich in natural wonders. Lucy Vincent and Squibnocket Beaches dazzle with dunes and rock formations not seen anywhere else. The hikes are exhilarating, not least to the Brickyard, where millions of bricks were made during the mid- to late 1800s for use in construction projects from Boston to New York (you might still find discarded red bricks along the rocky north shore). And then there's Menemsha, the charming fishing village where lobster rolls are best enjoyed with a seltzer from the world's cutest gas station. You'll see what I mean.

One of Chilmark's hidden gems is the Island Folk Pottery trail, where sculptor Bill O'Callaghan and his wife, potter and tile maker Heather Goff, host a whimsical path of curiosities in their gardens. Come at dusk and dance with the fireflies and fairies.

EDGARTOWN

WAMPANOAG NAME:
Nunne-Pog (Edgartown)
Tchepiaquidenet (Chappaquiddick)

There is much to explore in Edgartown's nooks and crannies. You have Edgartown proper, a parade of boutiques, old whaling captains' homes, and immaculate gardens that lead you to the iconic Edgartown Harbor Lighthouse. From there, take the minute-long ferry to Chappaquiddick, the island off the island. During the summer, when the crowds swell and it's easiest to get around without a car, cycling is the way to go. Ride over to the serene Mytoi Japanese garden for a contemplative stroll along its winding paths. Continue cycling over to East Beach for a picnic on the dunes. Then, take the ferry back over to the "big" island and cycle to Katama's flat fields, waving to the vintage biplanes taking off for joyrides as you bike back into town for a well-deserved ice cream.

OAK BLUFFS

WAMPANOAG NAME: Ogkeshkuppe

Oak Bluffs is the quintessential summer resort town, with its fudge shops and ice cream and souvenir T-shirts. It's fun to play tourist on Circuit Avenue, before going for a spin at the Flying Horses, the country's oldest operating carousel, opened in 1884. Celebrate the glory of grabbing the coveted brass ring with a frozen cocktail on the harbor.

Continue over to the waterfront for miles of beach playground. The town's most famous beach, Inkwell Beach, is a celebration of joy, culture, and community, from sunrise yoga to sunset porch sessions. The sea breeze drifts over to the campgrounds, where Illumination Night dazzles every August when thousands of lanterns cast a glow over the pastel gingerbread cottages.

VINEYARD HAVEN

WAMPANOAG NAME: Nobnocket

Charming Main Street has a little of everything, and it's the ideal place to relish an unhurried stroll with a scoop or two of ice cream. Veer out of town and you'll be rewarded with quiet discoveries: West Chop lighthouse on the northernmost tip of Tisbury (the town's official name), swimming at Lake Tashmoo or fishing at Eastville Point Beach, watching the ferries come and go.

The Martha's Vineyard Museum, housed in the old hospital on the hill, offers a fascinating curation of local history. It's a must-visit if only for Tim Laursen's solar-powered, kinetic *Sun Bird* sculpture, a fine example of Vineyard ingenuity.

MOSTLY OPEN
SOMETIMES CLOSED

WEST TISBURY

West Tisbury runs from the Caribbean-like Lambert's Cove in the north to the rough and tumble shores of the south; horse trails and meadows are a warm welcome to the up-island towns of the west. So peaceful, yet home to so much of island life, not least the farmers market, the Agricultural Fair every August, and Alley's General Store, the oldest retailer on the island.

While passing through town, tip your hat to one of its most unique personages. Nancy Luce (1814–1890) was the island's first celebrity. Poet, artist, businesswoman, and great lover and keeper of chickens, she bestowed names like Tweedle Dedel and Lebootie Ticktuzy on her banties, then immortalized their kinship in soul-wrenching poetry. Visit her gravestone in West Tisbury cemetery—you can't miss it.

Breakfast

Açai Bowl
with Island Dream Granola

AQUILA, AQUINNAH

Aquila owners Del and Jennifer Araujo met at college in Connecticut, bonding over a shared love of café life and dreaming of owning their own coffee shop one day. So, when the opportunity to take over a store at the Aquinnah cliffs came up, the couple jumped at the chance. There had to be locally roasted coffee, naturally, and supporting local artisans was also part of the plan. Today they offer a charming stop on the way to the cliffs or beach: wampum jewelry, pottery, art, snacks, and great local coffee. And they named it after Aquila, Latin for eagle, the constellation that can be seen above the cliffs in July and August.

There's something about starting the day with an açai bowl that makes you feel like you're on vacation, and perhaps that's why Aquila's signature rainbow-hued creations have become so popular. Jennifer's island-inspired granola is not too sweet, the perfect counterpart to vitamin-packed açai. The recipe makes more than you'll need, but leftover granola will keep for up to 2 weeks in an airtight container, and it's great to have on hand.

SERVES 4

3 cups rolled oats

1 cup raw almonds, chopped

1 cup dried banana chips, chopped

1 cup plus 2 teaspoons unsweetened grated coconut

½ cup raw pumpkin seeds

½ cup raw sunflower seeds

2 tablespoons plus 1 teaspoon chia seeds

¾ cup maple syrup

⅓ cup refined coconut oil, melted

1 heaping tablespoon local honey, such as Black Brook, plus more for the açai

¼ teaspoon salt, such as MV Sea Salt

2 cups frozen açai

4 bananas, peeled and sliced

8 strawberries, sliced

¼ cup blueberries

Preheat the oven to 250°F and line a large baking sheet with parchment paper.

In a large bowl combine the oats, almonds, banana chips, 1 cup coconut flakes, pumpkin seeds, sunflower seeds, and 2 tablespoons chia seeds. Stir in the maple syrup, coconut oil, 1 tablespoon honey, and salt, and mix to combine.

Spread the granola on the prepared baking sheet in an even layer. Bake, stirring every 15 to 20 minutes, until the granola is golden brown and fragrant, 1 hour to 1 hour 10 minutes. Remove from the oven and let the granola cool completely. It will continue to harden as it cools.

To make each açai bowl, spoon ½ cup frozen açai into a bowl, top with 1 of the sliced bananas, 2 of the sliced strawberries, a few blueberries, ½ cup of granola, ½ teaspoon of the remaining coconut flakes, and ¼ teaspoon of the remaining chia seeds. Drizzle with honey.

Blueberry Buttermilk Scones

ARTCLIFF DINER, VINEYARD HAVEN

Martha's Vineyard is spoiled with classic and cozy diners. Case in point: ArtCliff Diner, now in its eighth decade (the original owners Art Silva and Cliff Luce set up their dining car on Beach Road in 1943). The welcome is as warm as ever, thanks to owner Gina Stanley, whose kindness radiates out from the busy kitchen (with a team just as gracious). Vintage vinyl lunch counter seats and other retro decor add to the charm. You've got all the diner staples—hash 'n' eggs, malted buttermilk pancakes, and these crowd-favorite, big-as-a-plate blueberry scones. In the restaurant, the scones are stacked high on antique cake stands, but they don't last long. If they do sell out, you're still in luck—you can bake your own lofty scones in less than 30 minutes. Serve warm with butter, jam, and a hot refill. For sweet potato scones, omit the blueberries and include one roasted and mashed sweet potato.

MAKES 8 LARGE SCONES

3 cups all-purpose flour

¾ cup granulated sugar

1½ teaspoons baking powder

½ teaspoon baking soda

½ teaspoon kosher salt

1 stick (8 tablespoons) cold unsalted butter, cut into cubes

1 cup buttermilk

1½ teaspoons vanilla extract

Finely grated zest of ½ lemon

1 cup fresh or frozen blueberries

1 tablespoon light brown sugar or turbinado sugar

Confectioners' sugar for finishing

Preheat the oven to 375°F. Line 2 baking sheets with parchment paper. In the bowl of a stand mixer fitted with the paddle attachment, combine the flour, granulated sugar, baking powder, baking soda, and salt on low speed. Add the butter and incorporate until the mixture resembles little pebbles. (Alternatively, use your fingers to cut the butter into the dry ingredients.)

Add the buttermilk, vanilla extract, and lemon zest, and mix on low until just combined. (Or mix gently with a wooden spoon until just combined.) Fold in the blueberries with a wooden spoon. Scoop 8 equal portions and shape each into a round (about 5 inches in diameter) on the prepared pans, leaving 3 inches of space around each. Sprinkle with brown sugar. Bake until a toothpick inserted in the center comes out clean, 18 to 22 minutes. Cool on the pans for 5 minutes. Dust with confectioners' sugar.

Butternut Squash Quick Bread

NORTH TISBURY FARM, WEST TISBURY

You simply can't leave North Tisbury Farm without a treat. It may come in the form of a bouquet of rainbow flowers, picked from the garden beside the store, a perfect Goldbud nectarine, or perhaps some fancy butter to serve with this any-time-of-day loaf. Owner Rose Willett uses squash from her nearby Whippoorwill Farm for this quick bread, which is just that—quick to make for (almost) instant gratification, deliciously moist, and fragrant with autumnal spices. While the bread is cooling, whip salted butter with local honey to spread thickly over a slice (or two).

MAKES 1 LOAF

1 stick (8 tablespoons) unsalted butter, melted, or ½ cup vegetable oil, plus more for pan

2 cups all-purpose flour

1 cup granulated sugar

½ cup light brown sugar

2 teaspoons ground cinnamon

1 teaspoon ground cardamom

1 teaspoon baking soda

½ teaspoon baking powder

½ teaspoon ground nutmeg

½ teaspoon ground ginger

½ teaspoon kosher salt

1 cup store-bought or homemade butternut squash purée (see Tip)

2 large eggs

¼ cup full-fat sour cream

1 teaspoon vanilla extract

Preheat the oven to 350°F. Butter or oil a 9 by 5–inch loaf pan.

In a large bowl, whisk together the flour, sugars, cinnamon, cardamom, baking soda, baking powder, nutmeg, ginger, and salt. In a separate large bowl, whisk the melted butter, the squash purée, eggs, sour cream, and vanilla extract. Fold the dry ingredients into the wet with a silicone spatula until no dry spots remain.

Pour the batter into the prepared loaf pan and bake until the top is golden brown and a tester inserted into the center of the bread comes out clean, about 1 hour. Remove from the oven and cool in the pan.

Tip: To make your own squash purée, preheat the oven to 375°F. Line a baking sheet with parchment paper. Cut 1 butternut squash in half lengthwise, remove the seeds with a spoon, and brush the cut sides with olive oil. Roast, cut side down, for about 1 hour, or until very tender (a knife inserted in the flesh should slide through without any resistance). Remove from the oven and, when cool enough to handle, scoop the flesh into a blender and purée until smooth. Set aside 1 cup to go with the wet ingredients. Refrigerate leftovers in an airtight container for up to 1 week (use in muffins or pasta sauce).

Coffee Cake

ROSEWATER, EDGARTOWN

Meet you at Rosewater. The sweet year-round café is a favorite spot to catch up with friends and offers something for everyone: homemade cakes and bakes and freshly brewed Chilmark Coffee, breakfast and lunch to enjoy on the patio, and provisions to take with you on a picnic. Their light and buttery coffee cake with a brown sugar-cinnamon-nut swirl in the center has been a must-order for years. Plus, it's gluten-free. (If using standard cake flour in place of the gluten-free flour, go with 3½ cups.) The batter comes together in minutes, so pour yourself a hot brew to enjoy alongside for the perfect mid-morning pick-me-up.

MAKES ONE (10-INCH) CAKE; SERVES 8 TO 10

Filling

1 cup light brown sugar

¾ cup pecans, toasted and chopped

1 tablespoon ground cinnamon

Cake

3 sticks plus 2 tablespoons unsalted butter, at room temperature, plus more for pan

3¼ cups granulated sugar

4 large eggs

1½ teaspoons vanilla extract

1⅔ cups full-fat sour cream, at room temperature

Scant 4 cups Cup4Cup gluten-free flour, plus more for pan

2½ teaspoons baking powder

1 teaspoon kosher salt

Glaze

2 cups confectioners' sugar, sifted

¼ cup whole milk

1 teaspoon vanilla extract

Make the filling: Combine the brown sugar, pecans, and ground cinnamon in a medium bowl. Set aside.

Make the cake: Preheat the oven to 350°F. Butter and flour a 10-inch Bundt pan and tap out excess flour. Place the butter and sugar in the bowl of a stand mixer fitted with the paddle attachment. Beat on medium speed until light and fluffy, about 3 minutes. Add the eggs and vanilla extract and beat until fully incorporated. Add the sour cream and beat until incorporated, then scrape down the sides of the bowl. The batter will look lumpy, which is fine.

Whisk together the flour, baking powder, and salt in a large bowl. Gradually add the dry ingredients to the butter mixture and mix on low speed until smooth.

Scoop some of the cake batter into the prepared pan to reach one-third of the way up the sides of the pan. Using a spoon, make a channel all the way around the center of the batter. Fill the channel with the filling. Scoop the remaining batter on top to cover the filling.

Bake until the cake is lightly golden brown and a skewer inserted in the center of the ring comes out clean, about 1 hour 20 minutes. Cool in the pan for 20 minutes, then unmold onto a rack to cool completely.

Make the glaze: In a medium bowl, whisk together the confectioners' sugar, milk, and vanilla until smooth. Let the glaze thicken slightly, about 10 minutes. Drizzle the cooled cake with the glaze. Slice and serve.

Cranberry Maple Oat Scones

SCOTTISH BAKEHOUSE, VINEYARD HAVEN

It's easy to have that kid-in-a-candy-store feeling walking into the Scottish Bakehouse, with pies and brownies and cookies of all kinds and twenty or so other baked goodies on display. While waiting in line for coffee and shortbread or a breakfast sandwich, seek out the photos on the wall of Isabella White, who journeyed from Scotland and opened the year-round bakery in 1961.

Are the recipes still hers? Owner Daniele Barrick laughs, "Let's just say they used margarine back then, and we use quality ingredients." Indeed, everything is still made from scratch, with meat and produce from local farms and the bakery's own garden. Daniele, who took over in 2002, is only the third owner in the bakery's history, and her loyal team is family. Head baker Caitlin Crossland has been baking since the age of ten and has a seemingly endless supply of creativity. One morning she might whip up retro grasshopper bars, another day garlic knots. Inclusivity is key, with desserts for every dietary need tempting behind the counter. These tender, not-too-sweet scones are a nod to New England with cranberries and maple syrup, while oats and buttermilk throw back to their Scottish roots. Isabella would be proud.

MAKES 10 SCONES

2¼ cups
all-purpose flour

½ cup rolled oats

1 tablespoon
granulated sugar

1 tablespoon
baking powder

1 teaspoon kosher salt

2 sticks
(16 tablespoons) cold
unsalted butter, cubed

1⅔ cups frozen
cranberries (see Note)

2 large eggs,
lightly beaten

¼ cup buttermilk

½ cup maple syrup

1 teaspoon vanilla
extract

2 tablespoons
whole milk

1½ cups confectioners'
sugar

Preheat the oven to 350°F. Line 2 baking sheets with parchment paper and set aside. In the bowl of a stand mixer fitted with the paddle attachment, combine the flour, oats, granulated sugar, baking powder, salt, and cold butter. Mix on medium speed until the butter is the size of peas, about 1 minute. (Alternatively, use your fingers to cut the butter into the dry ingredients.) Add the cranberries and mix until just combined.

Whisk the eggs, buttermilk, ¼ cup maple syrup, and vanilla extract in a medium bowl. Add this liquid to the flour mixture in a thin stream while stirring with a wooden spoon. Stir until the dough just comes together; do not overmix.

Scoop 10 equal portions and shape each into a round (about 4 inches in diameter) on the prepared pans, leaving 2 inches of space around each. Bake until a toothpick inserted into the center comes out clean, about 30 minutes. Remove from the oven and cool on the pans on a rack.

Whisk the remaining ¼ cup maple syrup, milk, and confectioners' sugar in a small bowl until smooth. Drizzle over the cooled scones.

Note: If you can't find frozen cranberries, use dried cranberries and soak them in 3 cups water for 20 minutes to plump them.

Eidolon-Frosted Cinnamon Rolls

THE GREY BARN, CHILMARK

The Grey Barn greets you in true up-island fashion: a long dirt road, stone walls, chickens footloose and fancy-free. Magical moments await within the farmstand. The deep, toasty perfume of butter and sugar, a whiff of yeasty cheese, the meat counter that beckons for summer grilling or slow cooking when the days shorten. The farm, founded by Molly and Eric Glasgow in 2009, is an essential pit stop for many islanders, whether to pick up a burnished boule and wedge of buttercup-yellow cheese to serve with dinner or a glorious pastry for the morning after.

These lofty cinnamon rolls are perfect for a leisurely weekend. They are iced with Eidolon, their signature bloomy rind cheese that is both creamy and cakey. It gives the rolls a rich tang and bestows them with a sense of place. This uniquely Martha's Vineyard cheese, which changes flavor and hue with the seasons and pastures, is made in-house using organic milk from their own cows. If Eidolon is not available, substitute with cream cheese. Tangzhong is a no-fuss technique that ensures plushness and keeps the rolls fresh for days, if they last that long.

MAKES 8 ROLLS

Tangzhong

½ cup whole milk

3 tablespoons bread flour

Dough

⅔ cup whole milk, cold

2½ cups bread flour

1 teaspoon kosher salt

2 tablespoons granulated sugar

2 teaspoons instant yeast

4 tablespoons unsalted butter, at room temperature, plus more for greasing

Filling

1 tablespoon unsalted butter, melted

½ cup light brown sugar

1 tablespoon ground cinnamon

Finely grated zest of 1 orange

Icing

4 ounces Eidolon cheese or cream cheese

1½ cups confectioners' sugar, sifted

1 to 2 tablespoons whole milk

½ teaspoon vanilla extract

½ teaspoon kosher salt

Make the tangzhong: Combine the milk and flour in a small saucepan and whisk until no lumps remain. Place the saucepan over medium heat and cook the mixture, stirring with a wooden spoon regularly, until it is thickened and the spoon leaves lines on the bottom of the pan, 1 to 3 minutes. Remove from the heat and transfer to the bowl of a stand mixer fitted with a dough hook.

Make the dough: To the tangzhong, one at a time add the milk, flour, salt, granulated sugar, yeast, and butter (in this order); the heat from the tangzhong will warm the cold milk. Mix on low speed until the dough comes together. Increase the speed to medium-low and knead until the dough is smooth, elastic, and tacky, 10 to 12 minutes.

Shape the dough into a ball, place it in a bowl, and cover the bowl with a kitchen towel. Let the dough rise until puffy, just before it has doubled in size, 1 to 1½ hours.

Make the filling: While the dough is rising, put the melted butter into a medium bowl and add the brown sugar, cinnamon, and orange zest. Stir until the mixture is the texture of damp sand. Set aside.

Assemble the cinnamon rolls: Transfer the dough to a lightly buttered surface and press it into a 10 by 12–inch rectangle that is ½ inch thick. Sprinkle the filling evenly over the dough, covering all but a ½-inch strip along one long side.

Starting with the filling-covered long side, roll the dough into a log. For large, saucer-size cinnamon rolls, use a sharp knife to score the dough lightly into eight (1½-inch-thick) pieces; for smaller rolls, divide the log into twelve (1-inch-thick) pieces. Cut the dough at the score marks.

Line two large baking sheets with parchment paper. Place the cinnamon rolls on the baking sheets, spacing them so there are at least 2 inches between each roll and they are 2 inches away from the edges of the pans. To prevent them from unraveling while

they rise and bake, tuck the ends of the spirals underneath the rolls. Cover the cinnamon rolls with a reusable cover (or lightly greased plastic wrap) and allow to rise until they are puffy and the dough does not bounce back immediately when gently pressed, 45 to 60 minutes. While the rolls are rising, preheat the oven to 375°F.

Bake the cinnamon rolls for 14 to 18 minutes. If you prefer extra-soft rolls, bake for about 14 minutes (the rolls should be a light golden brown); if you prefer rolls with a bit more color and slightly firmer texture,

bake for about 18 minutes. Remove from the oven and let the rolls cool for 10 to 15 minutes before icing.

Make the icing: While the rolls cool, place the cheese in a small food processor or mini-chop and process until smooth, 1 to 2 minutes. Combine with the confectioners' sugar, 1 tablespoon milk, vanilla, and salt in a medium bowl and mix with a silicone spatula until smooth. If the icing feels too stiff to spread, add the remaining 1 tablespoon milk a little at a time until it reaches a spreadable consistency. Ice the cinnamon rolls and serve immediately.

Peach Poppy Seed Muffins

LITTLE ROCK FARM, VINEYARD HAVEN

Starting a weekend at the farmers market is a cherished ritual from June to October. The first stop for many is the Little Rock farmstand for a pint of summer gazpacho made with the ripest tomatoes, diamonds of sticky baklava, or the farm's famous muffins. In 1974, Debbie Koines, then twenty-one years old, began selling fruit pies with her childhood best friend at the Grange Hall (the original site of the market), always selling out of her inventory within the first hour. When Debbie met her husband, Peter, a few years later while working at The Black Dog Tavern, they established Little Rock Farm and expanded their offerings. "Inspiration comes from all around," says Peter. "Traveling, visiting farms and markets where different ingredients are available, and, of course, childhood memories. My family's recipes are a huge influence on my menus. But also the diversity of our island community: the original inhabitants, the European colonizers, the various waves of immigrants. I have strived to reflect these influences when crafting our menus."

Today, their children, Olivia and Nicholas, help run the market stand. "Being a member of the farmers market for over thirty years and watching it evolve has been very rewarding," continues Peter. "It's all about the relationships. Whether our customers return year after year or are first-time visitors, recent washashores, or locals, we know the market is an integral part of their Vineyard experience." These peach poppy seed muffins were their first signature creation and their popularity hasn't waned all these years later.

MAKES 12 MUFFINS

1 stick (8 tablespoons) unsalted butter, at room temperature

1 cup granulated sugar

½ teaspoon kosher salt

2 large eggs, lightly beaten

2 cups all-purpose flour

2 teaspoons baking powder

1 cup whole milk

1 teaspoon vanilla extract

2 medium ripe peaches, peeled, pitted, and diced

2 tablespoons poppy seeds

Sanding sugar for finishing

Preheat the oven to 400°F. Line a standard 12-cup muffin pan with paper baking cups.

In the bowl of a stand mixer fitted with the paddle attachment, beat the butter, sugar, and salt on medium speed until light and fluffy, 3 to 5 minutes. (Alternatively, you can mix the entire batter by hand.) With the mixer running, add the eggs one at a time, then mix on medium speed until thoroughly incorporated. Add the flour, baking powder, and ⅔ cup milk and mix on low speed until smooth, about 2 minutes. Add the remaining ⅓ cup milk and vanilla and mix for 1 additional minute, until combined. With a silicone spatula, fold in the peaches and poppy seeds.

Scoop the batter into the prepared muffin tins, filling them almost to the top. Sprinkle sanding sugar on top. Bake until the muffins are golden brown and a toothpick inserted comes out clean, 15 to 20 minutes. Remove the muffins from the tin and let cool on a wire rack.

Meg & Dan Athearn

In 1975, Jim and Debbie Athearn established Morning Glory Farm, and six years later they followed it up with the farmstand that still stands today. Morning Glory has grown to become the largest farming operation on Martha's Vineyard, with seventy acres of non-GMO fruits and vegetables, four acres of cut flowers, and over 250 acres of farmland managed by the family and used for livestock, including grassfed beef, pasture-raised pork, and poultry. The farm is now run by the next generation of Athearns, sons Simon and Dan and their wives, Robyn and Meg, with the same commitment to sustainable, ethical farming. Dan is the farm's machinery specialist and operations officer while Meg runs philanthropy and the farmers market operation. The farm's name comes from that special feeling of setting out for the day as the sun is rising with a full day's promise ahead of you, and that's apt for Dan and Meg. Their days may be long, but they're rewarded with spending time together as a family doing what they love most.

Dan: Any day that includes foraging, fishing, hunting, and cooking with what Meg's brought home from the market is a perfect Vineyard day for us.

Meg: I agree. I think a summer Saturday is our favorite day. Farmers market mornings are busy but happy. I love the social aspect of the market, demystifying ingredients and collaborating with our customers on recipes. You actually know which recipe the *New York Times* has just published, because that's what everyone will be buying the ingredients for.

Dan: After the market, Meg and the kids [Zeb, Clara, and Penelope] join me on the boat. Or we'll go foraging. The kids really love it. Depending on the season, we'll find wild strawberries, huckleberries, beach plums, blueberries, or mushrooms. Special treats.

Dinner could be anything from stripers we've caught that day to a clam boil, using the wilted veggies not sold at the market. We like to eat what others don't so much. Dogfish, false albacore, bluefish—as long as you handle it well, it's delicious. We'll invite friends over and make this bluefish dish that converts the most stubborn non-fish eaters: Spread fillets with mayonnaise and Dijon mustard, then top with thinly sliced onion, cherry tomatoes, and lemon thyme. Bake in a hot oven for a few minutes, then sprinkle with a tiny amount of sugar and broil to caramelize lightly. The sweetness offsets the robust flavor of the fish. It feels so satisfying making a meal for someone when you've put in the extra effort.

Meg: When the market winds down in the fall, clamming, foraging, and making a meal with that day's treasures is still our favorite way to spend a day. It's all about the experiences we forge together. We're so grateful for the land and sea that surround us.

Strawberry Sourdough Bread

MORNING GLORY FARM, EDGARTOWN

Few things are as sublime as a Morning Glory Farm strawberry. The date of the first harvest is as highly anticipated as summer ferry reservations; there's even a festival every June to celebrate. The strawberry season is short but the pleasures of this perfect fruit linger long. While strawberry shortcakes might be the default summer bake, this fragrant loaf created by head baker Teresa Kirkpatrick and head yeast baker Whitney Cleary should tempt you to try something new. Imagine a slice schmeared with homemade strawberry butter (!), or toasted and dipped into Honey Brûléed Brie (page 231). This recipe offers an excellent way to use up strawberries that have seen better days. Like all of Morning Glory Farm's made-from-scratch baked goods, this loaf stays true to the farm's ethos of making food that is simple yet exceptional.

It's best (and easiest) to use a digital scale to measure ingredients for sourdough accurately in grams. No need to get out all your measuring cups and spoons! An inexpensive banneton or proofing basket makes shaping and turning out the dough a breeze. If you love to bake, you'll get a lot of use out of these kitchen additions (not to mention that this bread is so delicious you're sure to make it multiple times).

MAKES 1 LOAF

Levain

65 g water

65 g bread flour

65 g ripe sourdough starter (see page 46)

Final Dough

115 g ripe hulled strawberries

330 g bread flour, plus more for work surface

20 g whole wheat flour

20 g rye or spelt flour

150 g levain (from Day 1)

200 g water

10 g kosher salt

All-purpose flour for work surface

Neutral oil for bowl

Day 1

Make the levain: Mix the water, bread flour, and sourdough starter in a medium bowl with a wooden spoon. Leave out for 8 to 10 hours at 75°F to 80°F. If your kitchen is cold, leave in the oven with the oven light on.

Day 2

Make the final dough: Pulse the strawberries in a food processor fitted with the metal blade to form a coarse and somewhat chunky mixture. Combine the strawberries, flours, levain, water, and salt in a large bowl. If the mixture seems dry, add water, 10 grams at a time, until the ingredients are just combined into a shaggy dough. Cover with a kitchen towel or reusable bowl cover and set aside to rest in the bowl for 15 to 20 minutes.

Use wet hands to pick up the dough, stretch it up, and fold it over the dough. Then rotate the bowl 180 degrees and repeat. Rotate the bowl 90 degrees and do another stretch and fold. Finally, rotate the bowl 180 degrees, do the last stretch and fold for four folds total. Turn the dough out onto a lightly floured surface and knead by hand for 5 minutes. Place the dough in a large bowl lightly coated with neutral oil and cover with a damp kitchen towel.

For the next 2 hours stretch and fold the dough as above every 30 minutes (four sets in total), covering the dough with a damp kitchen towel each time. After you are done, cover the dough with the damp towel and let the dough rest up to 2 hours. Gently remove the dough from the bowl, place on a well-floured surface, and shape into a round. This is a slightly sticky dough, so it is a good idea to keep a small pile of bench flour at hand to use during the shaping process. Don't add too much flour though, otherwise the bread can end up heavy. Using a bench scraper will also help ease the dough into shape.

Rest the dough, lightly covered, for 30 minutes. Do a final shape touch-up and place into a well-floured banneton (proofing basket) or well-floured bowl with the dough top side down. Cover with plastic wrap or place in a loose plastic bag and refrigerate for 8 to 12 hours.

RECIPE CONTINUES

Day 3

Preheat the oven to 475°F. Place a Dutch oven with a tight-fitting lid in the oven and heat it for at least 30 minutes. Remove the dough from the refrigerator. Place a large piece of parchment paper on a banneton and gently turn out the dough so that it rests on the parchment paper, smooth side up. Lift the parchment with the dough and carefully place it in the hot Dutch oven. Score the dough 1 to 2 times at a slight angle with a bread lame (razor blade tool) or very sharp knife no more than ¼ inch deep. Cover with the lid and bake for 20 minutes. Remove the lid and bake until the bread is golden brown, about 10 additional minutes. Carefully hold the sides of the parchment paper and lift the bread from the Dutch oven. Transfer with the paper to a rack. Cool for at least 1 hour before slicing.

Sourdough Starter

To make your own sourdough starter you'll need a digital scale. The process takes about 14 days.

Day 1

Mix 25 grams water and 25 grams all-purpose or bread flour in a clean jar, stir, and cover loosely with a lid or plastic wrap. Set aside to rest in a warm spot. An ambient temperature of 75°F to 80°F is best. If your kitchen is cold, leave the jar in the oven overnight with the oven light on.

Day 2

Mix 50 grams water and 50 grams all-purpose or bread flour into the mixture from day 1, making sure to stir well.

Days 3 to 6

Mix 50 grams of the mixture (now officially the beginnings of your starter), 50 grams water, and 50 grams all-purpose or bread flour in a clean jar, discarding the remaining mixture. Repeat this daily through day 6. (You don't have to use a clean jar after the initial transfer.)

Days 7 to 9

Repeat this process twice a day through day 9.

Day 10

The starter should be ready to use as long as it has been consistently doubling within 3 to 8 hours of being fed. If it hasn't doubled, continue this 50/50/50 procedure twice a day until you see vigorous growth. Depending on ambient temperature, as well as microbial levels, it can take 2 weeks or longer for the starter to reach maturity.

Initially there will be very little visible activity, but by day 3 you should see some bubbles and the mixture will have a slightly pungent but not unpleasant odor. It helps to put a rubber band around the jar, marking the level of the starter so that you can see it rising. There will not be the same amount of growth each day.

Lunch

The Best Tomato Sandwich

THE GARDEN FARM, WEST TISBURY

Lydia Fischer is the tomato whisperer. They grow twenty varieties on Flat Point Farm, selling pints in all colors, shapes, and sizes at the farmers market and at their honor-system farmstand at Menemsha crossroads, a stone's throw from Beetlebung Farm, where the Fischer family worked the land for generations. After studying at Berklee College of Music, Lydia returned to the island and fell in love with farming again—especially tomatoes. This commitment has earned Lydia the admiration of the farming community. "All of Lydia's produce is special," says Mallory Watts of Milkweed Farm, "but I really respect their dedication to a singular ingredient." Lydia's favorite way to enjoy tomatoes? "Honestly, nothing beats a tomato sandwich!" And while you might not need a recipe, this is a reminder that the best things in life are often the simplest, especially when you have beautiful ingredients made with loving care. Feel free to embellish with snipped chives, thinly sliced red onion, or thinly sliced cucumber.

MAKES 3 TO 4 SANDWICHES

1 baguette, sliced lengthwise

¾ cup mayonnaise or 6 tablespoons cold salted butter

¼ cup large basil leaves

2 balls mozzarella, thickly sliced

4 ripe tomatoes, thickly sliced

Flaky sea salt, such as MV Sea Salt

Spread the cut sides of both baguette pieces with mayonnaise or butter. Arrange the basil leaves on the bottom piece of bread and top with the mozzarella. Arrange the tomato slices on top of the mozzarella. Sprinkle generously with salt. Cover with the top piece of baguette. Cut into 3 or 4 portions and enjoy, preferably sitting in the sun without your phone to relish the moment.

Birria Grilled Cheese

MIDNIGHT TACO, OAK BLUFFS

Tuna tacos and striped bass ceviche bring Baja California vibes to Oak Bluffs. Owner Jordan Wallace learned to make the house special, birria tacos, from an abuela in SoCal. They are worth all the delicious mess. The meat is stewed long and slow, then stuffed into lard-brushed tortillas that are seared, pressed, and served with broth on the side for a decadent dip. This birria grilled cheese is Jordan's ultimate island mash-up, swapping out tortillas for The Grey Barn's sourdough (plus their Banneker cheddar-style cheese for the gooiest cheese pull). Grab a couple of cervezas from the package store and tuck in. This recipe makes a generous amount of birria, so you can make huge sandwiches. Leftover birria can be refrigerated in an airtight container for 5 days or frozen for up to 3 months for when the midnight munchies strike.

MAKES 4 TO 5 SANDWICHES

Beef Birria

4 pounds bone-in or boneless beef chuck roast (or any affordable, fatty cut such as stew beef or short rib)

Kosher salt and freshly ground black pepper

2 medium tomatoes, halved

1 large white onion, roughly chopped

1 head garlic, cloves peeled and crushed

4 dried guajillo chilies

3 dried arbol chilies

2 dried ancho chilies

20 mixed whole peppercorns

½ teaspoon white vinegar

4 cups beef broth

1 teaspoon Mexican oregano

1 teaspoon ground cumin

2 teaspoons chili powder

5 bay leaves

1 cinnamon stick

½ teaspoon apple cider vinegar

Pickled Onions

1 large red onion

3 cloves garlic, crushed

1 jalapeño, halved lengthwise

3 sprigs cilantro

5 to 7 mixed whole peppercorns

1 cup red wine vinegar

1 cup distilled white vinegar

½ teaspoon apple cider vinegar

3 bay leaves

2 teaspoons sea salt

1 teaspoon brown sugar

Crema

1 cup full-fat sour cream

2 cloves garlic

½ jalapeño

Finely grated zest and juice of ½ lime

½ cup cilantro leaves

Assembly

8 or 10 (¾-inch-thick) slices sourdough bread, such as The Grey Barn

1 pound cheese, such as Banneker, 4-Blend Mexican, or mozzarella, shredded

½ cup chopped cilantro

Make the birria: Heat a Dutch oven over medium heat. Season the beef with salt and pepper. Sear the beef, fatty side down, until it is browned and a crust forms, about 3 minutes. Repeat until browned on all sides, about 12 minutes total. Remove the beef to a bowl and add the tomatoes, onion, and garlic to the Dutch oven. Cook, stirring occasionally, until softened, about 7 minutes.

In a medium saucepan, toast the dried chilies and peppercorns over medium-low heat, stirring frequently. After 3 minutes, add 2 cups water and the vinegar and bring to a simmer. Simmer for 20 minutes to plump the chilies.

Transfer the tomato mixture and the chilies and their liquid to a blender and blend until smooth.

Pour the sauce into the Dutch oven. Add the beef, broth, oregano, cumin, chili powder, bay leaves, and cinnamon stick and bring to a simmer over low heat. Cover and cook, stirring occasionally, until the beef is tender enough to shred with a fork, 3 to 4 hours. Skim any foam that rises to the top while the beef is cooking. Add the apple cider vinegar and season with salt. Remove and discard the cinnamon stick and bay leaves. Remove the beef and shred with two forks (discard the bone if the beef was bone-in); place the shredded meat back in the liquid until ready to assemble the sandwiches.

Make the pickled onions: If you're using the pickles the same day, slice the onion very thin. If using them over the next few days, slice it ¼ inch thick. Place the onion, garlic, jalapeño, cilantro, peppercorns, vinegars, bay leaves, salt, and brown sugar in a large mason jar and shake vigorously to dissolve the salt and sugar. Allow to rest at room temperature for 30 minutes. (Leftovers can be refrigerated in an airtight container for up to 2 weeks.)

Make the crema: Blend the sour cream, garlic, jalapeño, and lime zest and juice in a blender until smooth. Add the cilantro and pulse until fully incorporated.

Assemble the sandwiches: Heat a large cast-iron skillet over medium-high heat. Brush 2 slices of bread on both sides with the cooking liquid. Toast the bread for 2 minutes, then flip and cook the other sides until crisp, 2 additional minutes. Place a generous amount of cheese on one slice. Add 2 tablespoons water to the pan, cover, and steam until the cheese has melted, about 2 minutes. Place a generous amount of shredded beef and some broth (and more cheese if you like) on top. Layer on pickled onions, crema, and chopped cilantro. Place the other slice of bread on top and press down firmly to achieve a crust on the bottom. Turn the sandwich and cook the other side until very crisp (a hard crust creates contrasting textures with the crispy bread and soft insides, similar to a birria taco). Repeat with remaining ingredients. Slice sandwiches and serve hot.

Brown-Butter Lobster Rolls

KATAMA GENERAL STORE, EDGARTOWN

If you're lucky, there will be lobster left over from your clambake (page 211), begging to be piled high into brioche rolls and gilded with nutty brown-butter mayo. Katama General Store's take on a lobster roll bridges the eternal debate of whether butter or mayonnaise reigns supreme; purists of either opinion should pay attention to the people—these are very often hailed as the island's best lobster rolls. If you didn't think it was possible to improve on a classic, well, you haven't tried this. A new Vineyard icon.

MAKES 4 SANDWICHES

Brown-Butter Mayo

8 tablespoons (1 stick) unsalted butter

1 cup good-quality mayonnaise

1 tablespoon lemon juice

½ teaspoon kosher salt

Pinch freshly ground black pepper

Vinaigrette

1 tablespoon plus 1 teaspoon apple cider vinegar

1 teaspoon honey

¼ teaspoon Dijon mustard

¾ teaspoon minced garlic

Pinch sumac

2 tablespoons plus 2 teaspoons avocado oil or other light oil

Kosher salt and freshly ground black pepper

Lobster Salad

1 pound cooked lobster meat

¼ cup Brown-Butter Mayo

2 tablespoons snipped chives

1 teaspoon celery seed

Pinch white pepper

Assembly

6 tablespoons unsalted butter, softened

4 split-top brioche rolls

1 cup shredded romaine lettuce

1 tablespoon celery leaves

1 tablespoon fresh tarragon leaves

Lemon wedges, for serving

Make the brown-butter mayo: Place the butter in a small saucepan and heat over low, swirling gently, until the butter solids melt and start to brown, 8 to 10 minutes. Don't step away as the butter can quickly burn. When the butter turns a hazelnut color, remove from the heat and cool completely. Pour into a small bowl and stir in the mayonnaise, lemon juice, salt, and pepper. Cover and refrigerate. (You'll have extra, but brown-butter mayo is incredible on any kind of sandwich. Refrigerate leftovers in an airtight container for up to 3 days.)

Make the vinaigrette: Whisk together the vinegar, honey, mustard, garlic, and sumac in a small bowl until smooth. Add the oil in a thin stream, whisking constantly, until emulsified. Season with salt and pepper.

Make the lobster salad: In a medium bowl, fold together the lobster, brown-butter mayo, chives, celery seed, and white pepper.

Assemble the rolls: Butter the rolls on all sides. Heat a medium skillet over medium heat and toast the rolls on all sides, 2 minutes.

Place the lettuce in a medium bowl and dress with the vinaigrette. Divide among the rolls. Divide the lobster salad among the rolls and garnish with the celery and tarragon leaves. Serve with lemon wedges.

Crab Cakes
with Hollandaise

THE BLACK DOG TAVERN, VINEYARD HAVEN

It's five p.m. on a bone-chilling February night. You're seated by the window of The Black Dog Tavern with a piping-hot mug of chowder, or perhaps a plate of crab cakes. The fireplace is toasty, the wooden floors creak with happy diners, and you can't imagine being anywhere else. That's how captain Robert Douglas must have felt shortly after opening Martha's Vineyard's first year-round restaurant on New Year's Day 1971. He named the beachfront tavern after his good girl, soon to be spotted on T-shirts and bumper stickers all over the world. The tavern is often the first port of call for those stepping off the ferry, seeking solace in the menu of restorative breakfasts, hearty sandwiches, and day-to-night comfort food—like these crab cakes. These can be served over a toasted English muffin, topped with poached eggs, and slathered with hollandaise, as shown here, stuffed into a sandwich, or served simply with a leafy salad. This is one dish that the Black Dog crew can't take off the menu or there'd be a mutiny.

MAKES 8 CAKES; SERVES 4

Crab Cakes

⅓ cup mayonnaise

1½ tablespoons Dijon mustard

1 tablespoon lemon juice

¼ cup minced red onion

¼ cup minced green bell pepper, patted dry

¼ cup minced red bell pepper, patted dry

1¼ pounds lump crabmeat, picked through for shells, drained

1 cup panko breadcrumbs

Kosher salt and coarsely ground black pepper

2 tablespoons unsalted butter

2 tablespoons canola or peanut oil

4 English muffins, split and toasted

8 poached eggs

Hollandaise

2 egg yolks

1 tablespoon fresh lemon juice

1 stick (8 tablespoons) unsalted butter, melted

Hot sauce

Kosher salt

Make the crab cakes: In a medium bowl, combine the mayonnaise, mustard, and lemon juice. Stir in the onion and bell peppers. Fold in the crab, being careful not to break up the meat. Gently stir in the panko. Season with salt and pepper.

Form the mixture into 8 cakes about 3 inches in diameter and 1½ inches thick. Place on a baking sheet, cover with plastic wrap, and refrigerate for 1 hour.

Preheat the oven to 200°F. Heat 1 tablespoon of the butter and 1 tablespoon of the oil in a cast-iron skillet large enough to hold 4 of the crab cakes and set over medium heat. Drop a pinch of crab mixture into the skillet. If it sizzles immediately, the butter and oil are hot enough.

Cook 4 cakes, turning once, until golden brown, 3 to 4 minutes per side. Transfer the cakes to a baking sheet and keep warm in the oven. Add the remaining 1 tablespoon butter and remaining 1 tablespoon oil to the skillet and cook the remaining crab cakes as above.

Place the English muffins cut sides up on 4 individual serving plates. Top each half with a crab cake. Place a poached egg on top of each.

Make the hollandaise: In a blender or food processor, blend the yolks and lemon juice until combined. With the motor running, add the melted butter in a thin stream through the feed tube. The sauce will emulsify and thicken. Season with hot sauce and salt. Drizzle the sauce over the eggs.

Falafel Bowls

LITTLE HOUSE CAFÉ, VINEYARD HAVEN

Though Martha's Vineyard is a small island, it has a world of flavors—a true microcosm of America. At Little House, Brook Katzen's cozy year-round restaurant, global comfort food informs the menu: Greek lamb burgers, red curry chicken kebabs, Indonesian gado gado, and verdant falafel bowls, all made from scratch. The always-popular falafel is the real deal, golden and crisp on the outside, fluffy and herbaceous within. Enjoy it over a chopped salad or in a wrap. Don't flip the page on the fry—using a wide, deep pan means you need only a small amount of oil that you can strain and reuse.

MAKES 24 FALAFEL BALLS; SERVES 4

1 pound dried chickpeas

1 pound dried fava beans

1 pound shallots, coarsely chopped

8 to 9 cloves garlic

Leaves of 1 bunch flat-leaf parsley

2 tablespoons kosher salt, plus more to taste

2 cups all-purpose flour

2 tablespoons baking powder

4 cucumbers, peeled and diced

2 medium tomatoes, diced

¼ medium red onion, finely diced

2 tablespoons fresh lemon juice

3 tablespoons extra virgin olive oil

½ cup mayonnaise

Vegetable oil for frying

4 cups mixed greens

Put the chickpeas and fava beans in separate large bowls and add cold water to cover by 4 inches. Soak in the refrigerator for at least 8 hours and up to 2 days. Drain and rinse thoroughly, keeping the beans separate.

In a food processor fitted with the metal blade, process the chickpeas until smooth, then transfer to a large bowl. Process the fava beans until smooth and add to the bowl. Continue with the shallots, 7 cloves garlic, and parsley, processing separately and adding to the bowl. Add 2 tablespoons salt to the bowl and mix well with your hands to combine.

Mix the flour and baking powder in a small bowl, then fold into the falafel mixture with your hands.

Line a baking sheet with parchment paper. Using a falafel or ice cream scoop, or a large spoon, gently shape the falafel into 24 portions, about 1½ tablespoons each. Place on the prepared baking sheet, cover, and refrigerate for 30 minutes.

Combine the cucumbers, tomatoes, and red onion in a large bowl. Whisk together 1 tablespoon lemon juice and the olive oil. Season with salt. Dress the cucumber salad with this and set aside.

Mince the 1 to 2 remaining garlic cloves. In a small bowl, combine the minced garlic and the remaining 1 tablespoon lemon juice. Stir in the mayonnaise and season with salt.

Line a large plate with paper towels. Pour 3 inches oil into a deep, wide cast-iron skillet or medium saucepan and bring to 350°F over medium-high heat.

Add as many balls of falafel as will fit without crowding. Fry until deep golden brown, about 2 minutes, then use tongs to turn the falafel and fry the other side until golden brown, about 2 additional minutes. Use a slotted spoon to transfer the falafel to the paper towels. Sprinkle with salt while hot. Repeat with the remaining falafel.

To serve, place 1 cup mixed greens in a bowl. Top with the cucumber salad and 6 falafel balls and drizzle with mayonnaise sauce. Repeat for the remaining bowls. Serve with warm pita.

Foul Moudammass

AALIA'S, OAK BLUFFS

Whether you're greeted by owners Joy Younan and Kelly Sciandra, or lured inside by the perfume of just-baked croissants, the feeling at Aalia's is the same: warm and welcoming. The menu is influenced by Joy's Lebanese background and Kelly's Italian roots, rewarding brunchers with fluffy eggs and hash browns that have reached iconic status, and lemony chicken sandwiches for lunch. Reminding us that brunch can be more than just bacon and eggs, Aalia's, named for a family friend, offers another taste of their shared Mediterranean heritage by way of Joy's mother's recipe for foul moudammass, an Egyptian staple that's made to be scooped up with warm pita. Though it requires a moment of foresight— soaking the beans overnight—the dish is largely hands-off. Serve it alongside your favorite mezze after a lazy morning at the beach.

SERVES 4

1 cup dried fava beans

5 cloves garlic

1 tablespoon kosher salt

½ cup fresh lemon juice (from 3 lemons)

Extra virgin olive oil for drizzling

2 scallions, chopped

¼ cup minced flat-leaf parsley leaves

Flat-leaf parsley sprigs, tomato roses, and olives for garnish

Warm pita for serving

Rinse the fava beans. Place 5 cups water in a large bowl. Add the beans, cover, and soak at room temperature for 8 to 12 hours.

Drain and rinse the beans in a colander and transfer to a large pot with 3 cups water. Bring to a boil over medium heat, then cover, reduce the heat to low, and cook until soft, about 1½ hours.

Pound the garlic with the salt in a mortar and pestle, or mash together with the side of a knife on a cutting board, then transfer to a small bowl and mix with the lemon juice. Stir the garlic mixture into the beans.

Divide the beans among 4 individual serving dishes. Drizzle with olive oil, sprinkle with scallions and minced parsley, garnish with parsley sprigs, tomato roses, and olives, and serve warm or at room temperature with warm pita.

Hot Lobster Rolls

GARDE EAST, VINEYARD HAVEN

There are few dreamier places to be on a summer afternoon than Garde East's deck overlooking Vineyard Haven marina. It's a feast for the eyes as well as the appetite, with a bountiful menu of local seafood from crudo to luxe fish sandwiches. It's hard to pass up the classic buttery lobster rolls with huge chunks of succulent lobster. Pass the potato chips.

MAKES 4 SANDWICHES

6 tablespoons unsalted butter

4 split-top brioche rolls

14 ounces cooked claw, knuckle, and tail lobster meat, picked over for shells

Kosher salt and freshly ground black pepper

1 cup frisée lettuce, chopped

1 teaspoon snipped chives

Melt 2 tablespoons butter in a medium skillet over medium heat. Toast both sides of the buns in the butter, about 2 minutes. Remove.

Wipe the skillet clean and melt the remaining 4 tablespoons butter over low heat. Add the lobster meat and sauté until warmed through, about 2 minutes. Season with salt and pepper.

Put lettuce in the bottom of each roll. Divide the lobster meat among the rolls and place on top of the lettuce, then garnish with chives.

How to Build the Perfect Sandwich
(+ Your Sandwich Needs This Garlic Aioli)

MO'S LUNCH, OAK BLUFFS

At Mo's Lunch, the sandwich is an art form. Tucked inside the PA Club, restaurateurs and friends Maura Martin and Austin Racine have created a cult following with their rock star sandwiches and equally magnificent desserts by Korilee Connelly. So, what makes their sammies so special? Maura, take it away . . .

"At Mo's, we don't care for a dry sandwich. We believe one thing that separates the at-home sandwich from the sandwich-shop sandwich is the amount of sauce. At home, we all play it safe, going light on the mayo and mustard, afraid to make the sandwich too soggy, too messy, or maybe we're keeping our calories in check. But when you order a sandwich out, it typically comes loaded with condiments, and this is what makes it especially tasty.

"Next are the ingredients and how you layer them. A basic sandwich may include sliced bread or a roll spread with butter or sauce, topped with lettuce/tomato/onion, and some meat and cheese. On a *good* sandwich, your bread is sturdy enough to support a generous slathering of condiments—and they will be generous. When the sauce is creamy (like our house garlic aioli, see recipe), make sure to balance out that richness with something tangy, spicy, or sour. Pickles, of course, but don't forget hot pepper relish, chutney, or vinegar. The same applies if you're using a fatty, salty protein. Mortadella, salami, and ham all cry out for something zesty.

"Now consider the vegetables. Raw vegetables add the crunch factor. The basics are great, but don't forget cucumbers, radishes, or cabbage. Roasted vegetables are softer and deeper in flavor and can stand in for meat. There are innumerable varieties of cheese and imitation meats that you could choose to be the star of your sandwich creation. And don't forget to season every layer of meat and vegetables with salt and freshly ground black pepper.

"The options are endless, but to construct a top-notch sandwich, play to every note of your palate—sweet, salty, sour, bitter, umami. Have a good mix of textures—soft, crunchy, luscious—and we beg you: do not go light on the sauce. This is key.

"One last thing. There's something about letting a sandwich get to know itself before you bite into it. When you wrap a sandwich, the bread, the meat, the veggies, and the sauce all become one, stronger together than they are alone. In one bite, you're left feeling that, yes, the humble sandwich is indeed a perfect meal."

Mo's Garlic Aioli
MAKES 2 CUPS

3 egg yolks

1 tablespoon Dijon mustard

5 cloves garlic

¼ cup lemon juice (from 2 lemons)

Kosher salt and freshly ground black pepper

1 cup neutral oil, such as canola or avocado oil

In a food processor fitted with the metal blade (or using an immersion blender), pulse the egg yolks, mustard, garlic, lemon juice, and seasoning of salt and pepper until combined. Process while adding the oil in a thin stream, then continue until the mixture is thick and creamy. Aioli will keep in the refrigerator in an airtight container for up to 4 days. Enjoy it on a sandwich, with fries and smashed potatoes, or as a dressing for Caesar and potato salads.

Shrimp & Cheesy Grits

BISCUITS, OAK BLUFFS

At their cozy and ever-popular seasonal brunch café opposite the Oak Bluffs harbor, Martha's Vineyard local Chris Arcudi and Jersey girl Celeste Elser have been welcoming regulars with Southern comfort food since 2001. Genuine hospitality is reflected in the good vibes (and lines out the door). Chicken and waffles and lofty biscuits and gravy jostle alongside New England classics like cod cakes Benedict and linguiça hash. Shrimp and grits are another favorite. Juicy shrimp snuggle into a bed of velvety, cheesy grits—satisfyingly rich and homey. Don't forget a shake of Tabasco if you like a kick. If you can manage, save room for their famous cinnamon rolls. Luckily, the colorful gingerbread cottages are just behind the café, so you can walk off your meal.

SERVES 4

1 cup stone-ground grits

1¾ cups shredded sharp cheddar cheese

4 tablespoons unsalted butter

Kosher salt and freshly ground black pepper

1 cup blackened seasoning

1 pound jumbo shrimp, peeled, deveined, and tails removed

Extra virgin olive oil for searing

1 clove garlic, minced

¼ cup jarred roasted red peppers, drained and diced

Chopped scallions for garnish

In a medium saucepan, bring 4 cups water to a rolling boil over medium-high heat. Add the grits and lower the heat to a simmer. Cook, stirring frequently, until smooth and not gritty, 20 to 25 minutes. Stir in the cheddar cheese and 2 tablespoons of the butter and season with salt and pepper.

Pat the shrimp dry with paper towels. Set aside 1 teaspoon of the blackened seasoning. Place the remaining blackened seasoning in a medium bowl and dredge the shrimp in the seasoning. Heat a thin film of olive oil in a large, heavy-bottomed skillet over medium heat. Add the shrimp and garlic and sauté until the shrimp are just cooked, 1 to 2 minutes. Add the remaining 2 tablespoons butter, the roasted red peppers, and the remaining 1 teaspoon blackened seasoning. Toss to combine and coat the shrimp, about 30 seconds. Spoon the grits into individual serving bowls, top with shrimp, and garnish with scallions. Serve hot.

Tuna Poke Bowls

Owner and chef Everett Whiting is passionate about local fish, proudly displaying the names of captains and boats alongside their catches to help educate customers and connect them with purveyors. There's no better way to enjoy ruby red tuna fresh off the boat than in the popular poke bowl. Traditionally, poke is sold by the pound to enjoy with friends at the beach; at The Fish House, it's served over sushi rice with lots of colorful accompaniments and just as beach-worthy.

SERVES 4

1 pound fresh tuna

1½ teaspoons sriracha

½ teaspoon lime juice

1½ teaspoons wasabi powder

1 (1-inch) piece ginger, peeled and grated

1 large clove garlic, grated

1¼ cups tamari

¼ cup toasted sesame oil

Cooked sushi rice

Garnishes

Thinly sliced avocado

Wakame salad

Pickled ginger

Wasabi mayonnaise

Tobiko

Onion rings

Black sesame seeds

Remove any skin, bloodline, or silver skin from the tuna. Cut into ¼- to ½-inch cubes. Keep refrigerated.

In a medium bowl combine the sriracha and lime juice. Whisk in the wasabi powder until dissolved. Whisk in the ginger, garlic, tamari, and sesame oil.

Gently toss the tuna in the sauce. Serve over sushi rice and garnish as desired.

Beet & Goat Cheese Stack v 16.50
balsamic glaze, mixed micro greens, ch
pistachio

Burrata & Arugula   17.50
balsamic truffle glaze, heirloom tomato, b
add toasted sourdough bread 3.50

co Curry Butternut Squash Soup v
ped w/sunflower seeds & micro greens
add toasted sourdough bread*** 3.50

room & Smoked Gouda Tart v 19.50
cheese, charred onion, thyme, truffle oil.
d w/arugula

n Short Rib Tacos -GFO-   19.50
slaw, radish, pepper, cilantro, in flour street
is. Cucumber salad on side. 2 per order.
d 3rd taco*** 8.50

Salmon Wellington   36.50
w/dill fingerling potatoes & toasted sesame
asparagus

Chicken Pot Pie   27.50
Traditional w/root veggies

Vegan Curry Pot Pie v 24.50
leeks, root veggies & cranberries

Polenta Stack v GF 24.50
medley of mushrooms, sauteed spinach,
chive oil

ACCOMPA

LIG

MAI

Vegan Lobster Rolls

THE PAWNEE HOUSE, OAK BLUFFS

Vegan-ish comfort food is one way to describe the offerings at The Pawnee House. A cozy spot with killer cocktails is another. Owners Debbie and Alex Cohen have created something special in what was once a department store that belonged to Alex's grandfather. "There's so much history with this building," beams Alex. The Pawnee House was first a grand Victorian hotel on Circuit Avenue, opened in 1872. After time took its toll, the hotel was dismantled and the ground floor divided into shops. In 1930, the current restaurant space welcomed the original Giordano's Italian restaurant, now on Lake Avenue. In 1949, Alex's grandfather Ben and his brother George stopped in Oak Bluffs for the day, en route to Nantucket. They must have liked what they saw because they decided to settle, first opening an army surplus store, then a clothing and furniture store. The building remains in the family to this day.

While the menu offers delectable options for all, such as red beans and rice, chicken pot pie, and salmon Wellington, Debbie has fun creating could've-fooled-me vegan twists on seaside favorites, like crab cakes and these lobster rolls that are popular with beach picnickers. And those cocktails? That's where Alex unleashes his infatuation with tiki drinks, crafting masterful concoctions with island ingredients and rare liquors. A recent libation included a Mermaid Farm feta brine wash with an MV Sea Salt rim. It doesn't get much more neighborly than that.

MAKES 4 SANDWICHES

2 (14-ounce) cans hearts of palm, drained

1 tablespoon avocado oil

2 tablespoons smoked paprika

½ teaspoon Old Bay seasoning

Kosher salt and freshly ground black pepper

2 tablespoons vegan (or regular) mayonnaise

1 rib celery, minced

2 tablespoons chopped fresh dill

2 tablespoons drained capers, roughly chopped

½ teaspoon celery seeds

1 tablespoon snipped chives, plus more for garnish

½ teaspoon garlic powder

Finely grated zest of 1 medium lemon

1 tablespoon fresh lemon juice

4 split-top hot dog buns

1 tablespoon vegan (or regular) butter, melted

1 lemon, cut into 4 wedges

Preheat the oven to 400°F. Cut the hearts of palm into nonuniform 1-inch shapes (to resemble lobster meat). In a large bowl, toss the hearts of palm pieces with the oil, smoked paprika, and Old Bay, and season with salt and pepper. Spread evenly on a baking sheet, and bake for 8 to 10 minutes, until heated through. Remove and cool.

In a medium bowl, combine the mayonnaise, celery, dill, capers, celery seed, 1 tablespoon chives, garlic powder, and lemon zest and juice. Add the hearts of palm and stir to combine. Taste and season with salt and pepper.

Heat a medium skillet over medium heat. Brush the rolls all over with butter. Toast both sides, about 2 minutes total. Remove from the heat and evenly divide the hearts of palm mixture among the buns. Garnish with chives and serve each with a lemon wedge.

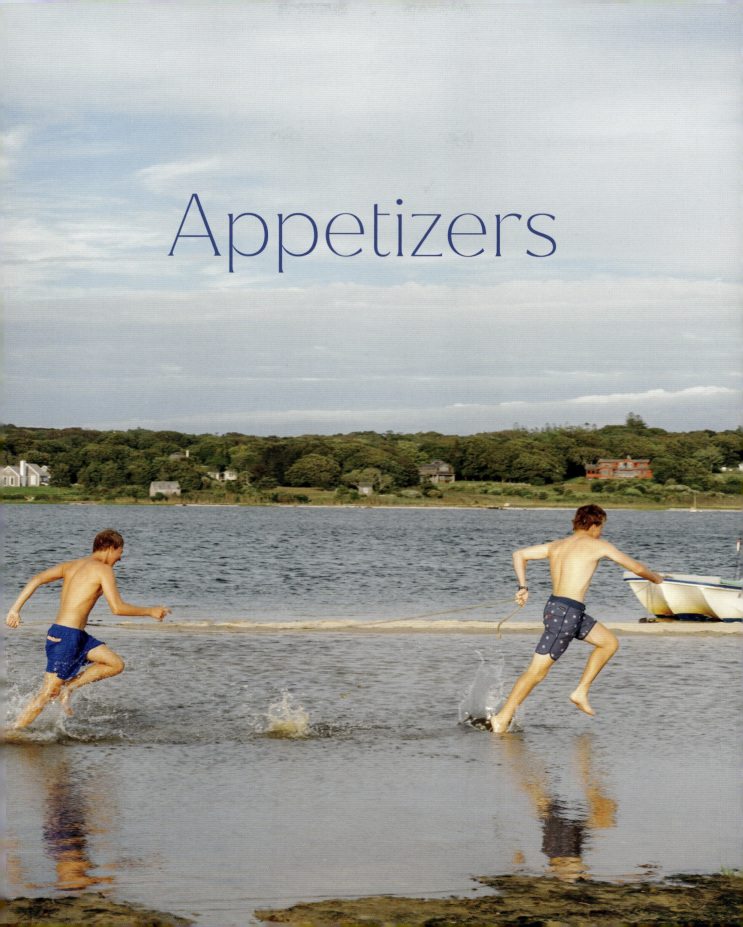

Appetizers

Carrot Dip

JOAN NATHAN, CHILMARK

Joan Nathan has traveled and lived all over the world, from France to Israel, New England, and Washington, D.C., with summers spent on Martha's Vineyard for almost 50 years. On a visit to Sydney, Australia, she fell in love with the carrot dip at the European-inspired deli diner Lox Stock & Barrel in Bondi Beach, and she has been making it back on the island ever since for dinner parties and for Rosh Hashanah, when sweet foods traditionally welcome the new year. Enjoy any time with fresh challah or crackers. The recipe is adapted from Joan's cookbook *A Sweet Year*.

SERVES 4 TO 6

2 tablespoons extra virgin olive oil

1 pound (about 6 large) carrots, peeled and cut into bite-size pieces

½ small red onion, cut into chunks

2 cloves garlic, thinly sliced

2 tablespoons chopped cilantro or flat-leaf parsley leaves, plus whole leaves for garnish

1 tablespoon fresh lemon juice

1 tablespoon honey, or to taste

1 teaspoon ground coriander

Kosher salt and freshly ground black pepper

Harissa to taste

Heat the olive oil in a large, heavy-bottomed skillet over medium heat and add the carrots, onion, and garlic. Cook until the carrots are tender enough to pierce with a fork, about 15 minutes. Add a touch of water if the carrots are looking dry. While the carrots are cooking, stir in the chopped cilantro, the lemon juice, the honey, and the coriander. Season with salt, pepper, and harissa. Remove from the heat.

When the carrots have cooled, purée in a blender until smooth. Transfer to a bowl, cover, and refrigerate for at least 6 hours, stirring occasionally, so that the flavors blend. Garnish with the cilantro leaves just before serving.

Joan Nathan

Cookbook author, food historian, and journalist Joan Nathan has been spending summers and then some on Martha's Vineyard with her family since the mid-1970s. Regarded as the matriarch of Jewish cooking, Joan has written and photographed many of her cookbooks in her Chilmark kitchen, including her latest, *A Sweet Year,* a cookbook for children, and *My Life in Recipes: Food, Family, and Memories,* her memoir with recipes. Joan divides her time between Washington, D.C, and Martha's Vineyard.

My perfect day on the Vineyard is a leisurely one. I'll wake up very early, and stay in bed reading—I love to read in bed. For breakfast, it's coffee and homemade granola, or cherry tomatoes and basil from my deck with eggs. And Mermaid Farm feta, which I always have in my fridge.

I'm quickly off to tennis in Chilmark, then back home for lunch I make salad from the garden or with lettuces from North Tabor Farm. I don't love lunch, but I do love salad as a midday meal.

Exploring this island, whether hiking or cycling or swimming, is one of my favorite things. I prefer to go to the beach in the late afternoon, so I head to my local beaches, Spring Point or Great Rock Bight, swimming into the sunset.

I like going to the Vineyard's feast of parties around different parts of the island, to pop-ups, or to intimate dinners at people's homes. This tiny island is so richly varied with people, and the venues are beautiful and interesting. If I go out to eat with friends, perhaps before a movie or a play, it's to State Road, Chef Deon's Kitchen, Chilmark Tavern, or the Outermost Inn. If I'm hosting, we might start with the Carrot Dip (opposite) and usually some fish, which I pick up at Larsen's or from Buddy Vanderhoop in Menemsha. We'll finish with a fresh pie or a crisp I've made of summer fruits like raspberries, rhubarb, or peaches from my garden (as long as the crows haven't grabbed the peaches!).

But also, my perfect Vineyard day could finish with a sunset dinner at Lambert's Cove Beach with my grandchildren. And every summer, I treat myself to a hot fudge sundae at Mad Martha's. It tastes just like the sundaes of my childhood.

Chicken & the Deviled Egg

BLACKWATER FARM, WEST TISBURY

Deviled eggs are the ultimate potluck food, and Vineyarders sure do love a potluck. This playful recipe is an ode to Blackwater Farm, whose friendly chickens welcome visitors to the farmstand, which is stocked with eggs, veggies, and delectable meats year-round. Making crispy chicken skin using the easy method below yields a bonus: schmaltz, or delicious chicken fat. When the weekend comes, fry your eggs in that liquid gold for extra flavor. For forty years, farm owners Debby Farber and Alan Cottle have been raising chickens, as well as cows and pigs, on their farm off Lambert's Cove. Every visit is a delightful surprise. There may be abundant bouquets of basil one day, tiny potatoes the size of marbles another. And always beautiful, farm-fresh eggs.

MAKES 12 PORTIONS; SERVES 6

6 hard-boiled eggs

3 tablespoons mayonnaise

1 teaspoon Dijon mustard

1 teaspoon apple cider vinegar, pickle juice, or kimchi juice

1 to 2 shakes hot sauce

Kosher salt and freshly ground black pepper

Skin from 4 chicken thighs, cut into twelve 1-inch squares

1 tablespoon snipped chives

Peel and halve the eggs. Remove the yolks and place in a small bowl. Add the mayonnaise, mustard, vinegar, and hot sauce and mash with a fork until smooth and combined. Season with salt and pepper.

Transfer the yolk mixture to a piping bag (or a zip-top bag with a corner snipped off). Pipe the mixture into the egg whites.

Arrange the skins in a single layer in a deep, wide microwave-safe container (not plastic). Set the microwave power setting to 30 percent and microwave for 8 minutes. Flip the skins with tongs, then return to the microwave and repeat the process. Carefully remove the container—it will be hot—and use tongs to transfer the skins to a plate lined with paper towels to drain. Season with salt. (Cool the rendered fat to room temperature, transfer to an airtight container, and refrigerate.)

Place a piece of crispy chicken skin on top of each egg and garnish with the chives.

Clams Cracktino

CLAMBULANCE, VINEYARD HAVEN

"If you're on island, make them after a long day at the beach. If you're in the city, make them after a long day at work." Sound advice from Beau Begin, who started Clambulance to share his love of raw bar with the Vineyard. He even shows up to events in his decked-out Clambulance van, complete with emergency raw bar kit (pass the mignonette, stat!). Beau is passionate about supporting the local seafood industry, and his sumptuous bars always feature an assortment of Vineyard oysters and clams, so guests can geek out at the variances that even a small island can produce. Make these delectable clams, Beau's take on clams casino, next time you need to avert a shellfish crisis.

SERVES 4

16 littleneck clams

½ sleeve Town House crackers

1 tablespoon unsalted butter, melted

1 to 2 teaspoons grated Pecorino Romano

½ teaspoon onion powder

½ teaspoon chopped flat-leaf parsley leaves

Tabasco sauce for serving

Preheat the oven to 350°F. Shuck the littlenecks and return each clam to a half shell (discard the other half). Put the shells on a baking sheet.

Pulverize the crackers in a food processor fitted with the metal blade and transfer to a medium bowl. Add the butter, Pecorino, onion powder, and parsley and stir to combine. Spoon the mixture over the littlenecks; the clams should be lightly covered.

Bake until the topping is golden, 13 to 15 minutes. For a deeper color, broil for 1 to 2 minutes, watching carefully so the topping does not burn. Serve with Tabasco.

Fried Silversides

SMOAK BBQ, CHILMARK

"French fries with eyes!" There's no more apt description of this utterly Vineyard snack, and we have Ann Khoan to thank. Ann and her husband, Tim Laursen, both cooks and artists, along with their friend Betsy Carnie, head chef at the Martha's Vineyard Public Charter School, netted and fried these silversides (tiny fish that swim in the shallows around Menemsha) right on the beach on a late-summer afternoon. Hot, crisp, and salty, they need nothing more than a cold beer and a dip in Old Bay mayo. It's an idyllic gathering with friends, demonstrating that you don't need much to create something memorable.

"Silversides are fun to eat, they're good for you, and they're a local food that many people don't even know about," says Tim. With the fire going, their two-year-old son husked Morning Glory Farm corn for Ann to grill alongside. The perfect send-off to summer.

These friends have more in common than just good times with good food. Tim and Ann's Smoak BBQ catering business combines a love of live-fire cooking with the mindfulness that comes from patiently feeding a flame for hours. Betsy brings similar intentionality to her school kitchen, encouraging students to be curious about food and helping them connect to local ingredients and the community around them.

This is a method more than a recipe; consider it an invitation to head for the nearest beach with friends, build a fire, and get frying.

Neutral oil

Potato starch

Cornstarch

Fresh silversides

Sea salt

Old Bay seasoning

Mayonnaise

Heat the oil in a large pot or wok to 350°F to 365°F. If you don't have a thermometer, to test the temperature drop a cube of bread in the oil; if it turns golden brown in about 15 seconds, your oil is ready for frying. In a large bowl, mix the starches together.

Working in batches so as not to overcrowd the pot, dredge the silversides in the starch mixture, shake off any excess, then add to the oil. Stir with a skimmer so the silversides don't stick together.

Fry until pale golden brown, 1 to 2 minutes, then remove with the skimmer and place on a platter. Sprinkle with salt immediately and dig in.

For the Old Bay mayo, combine 2 teaspoons Old Bay for every 1 cup mayonnaise in a small bowl. Serve alongside the fried fish.

Tip: If silversides aren't available where you are, use the same dredge and fry method for any other small seafood—tiny shrimp, calamari, or bay scallops. Adjust the cooking time accordingly.

Halibut Aguachile

THE COVINGTON, EDGARTOWN

The Covington is a love letter to the island's farming and fishing community. "We try to be as local as possible," says chef Alex Said, who sources from The Net Result, The Grey Barn, Beetlebung Farm, and Fork to Pork, among others. The menu is driven by intentional cooking. Take the halibut aguachile, for example. Alex uses the entire halibut: the belly and collar become a stunning centerpiece to share with friends, and offcuts from filleting are incorporated into this refreshing and colorful appetizer. "We want to honor the principles of nose-to-tail butchery, seeing that every part of the fish is used," he says. "In breaking down the whole fish, we get to experience firsthand what minimizing waste can look like, so the menu is really a combination of creativity and efficiency." All of this reflects the unique culture they've cultivated. "It's good vibes when you walk into The Covington; we support one another and work together seamlessly. Sustaining that feeling is what makes me most proud of being the chef here."

SERVES 4

2 cups distilled white vinegar

2 cups apple cider vinegar

½ cup sugar

3 cloves garlic, peeled and crushed

1 tablespoon coriander seed

1 bay leaf

10 Fresno peppers, seeded and sliced into thin rings

3 tablespoons pepitas

Canola oil for frying

2 tablespoons chili lime powder, such as Tajin or Valentina

1 English cucumber, unpeeled

4 ounces halibut, finely diced

2 tablespoons minced red onion

3 tablespoons minced fresh cilantro

2 teaspoons lime juice

1 teaspoon extra virgin olive oil

2 teaspoons kosher salt

1 teaspoon freshly ground black pepper

Agave syrup for finishing

Flaky sea salt, such as Maldon, for finishing

In a medium saucepan, combine the vinegars, 1 cup water, the sugar, garlic, coriander, and bay leaf and bring to a boil. Simmer until sugar is dissolved. Place the peppers in a medium heatproof jar with a lid and pour the hot pickling liquid over them. Cool to room temperature, then cover and chill for 24 hours before using. Cut 12 slices of pickled peppers into small dice and reserve. (You won't need all of the pickled peppers. Leftovers will keep in the refrigerator for 1 month. Add them to sandwiches and salsas.)

Place the pepitas in a small pan and add oil to cover generously. Place over high heat and cook, stirring constantly. When the pepitas float to the top and start to color, strain them, transferring the oil to a heatproof airtight container. Transfer the pepitas to a cutting board, toss with the chili lime powder, and roughly chop; set aside in a small bowl. (Store the oil at room temperature for up to 3 days. It can be used for frying other items.)

Slice the cucumber into 24 thin slices and finely dice a 2-inch piece. Place 6 cucumber slices on each individual serving plate. In a small bowl, combine the diced cucumber, halibut, pickled peppers, red onion, cilantro, lime juice, olive oil, salt, and pepper. Mix thoroughly and spoon on top of the cucumber on each plate. Top with the pepitas. Drizzle with agave and sprinkle with Maldon salt to finish.

Lobster Bao

JESSICA MASON, CHILMARK

You might assume seafood is Martha's Vineyard's number one export off the island, or maybe *Jaws* souvenirs. Sadly, it's garbage. Increasingly concerned by climate change and alarmed by the number of single-use takeout containers clogging up our oceans and landfills, local entrepreneur Jessica Mason decided to tackle the issue by starting Island Eats, a program that takes a page from reusable milk bottle programs of the past and replaces disposable containers at eateries across the island with reusable bowls and cups.

"I love this island and I wanted to find a way to tackle the buildup of trash that threatens our natural environment," says Jessica. "Reuse is the way forward." The program functions like a library: When you pick up your takeout from one of the partner cafés and restaurants, scan the container to borrow it using the free app, enjoy your food or drink, and return the container when you're done. Jessica and the Island Eats team then commercially wash and sanitize the containers and redistribute them. The program is free to use and open to all, and it helps to reduce the seasonal swell of trash.

Growing up in Australia, this recipe is an homage to both of Jessica's island homes. "Really delicious Chinese food is abundant in Sydney," she shares. "There is always seafood stir-fried with ginger and scallion on the menu, so when I was pining for Sydney and the amazing meals from my childhood, I decided to recreate the flavor with local lobster and bao buns, as a fun twist on our island's ubiquitous lobster rolls. They are a hit with my family and we love making them for friends."

MAKES 10 BUNS

Kosher salt

2 (1½-pound) live lobsters

1 tablespoon soy sauce

¼ teaspoon sesame oil

Pinch sugar

1 teaspoon white pepper

10 frozen bao buns

2 tablespoons vegetable oil

1 (2-inch) piece ginger, peeled and cut into matchsticks

4 scallions, thinly sliced, whites and greens separated

2 tablespoons shaoxing cooking wine or dry sherry

Garlic chives or regular chives, cut into 1-inch pieces

Chili crisp (optional), for serving

Put 2 inches of water into a pot large enough to hold both lobsters without crowding. Salt the water, fit a steamer basket or rack inside the pot, and bring the water to a rolling boil.

Add the lobsters, reduce the heat to medium, and cover. Steam until the meat pulls away from the shell but the lobsters are not fully cooked, about 8 minutes. Meanwhile, in a small bowl, combine the soy sauce, sesame oil, sugar, and white pepper.

Remove the lobsters and allow to rest until cool enough to handle. Remove the body, tail, and claw meat from the shells, cut into bite-size pieces, and set aside.

Clean the pot used to steam the lobsters and add 2 inches of water. Line a steamer with parchment paper and place in the pot. Bring the water to a boil and place the frozen bao buns in the steamer (do not thaw the bao). Cover the pot and steam until soft and pillowy, 10 to 15 minutes.

While the buns are steaming, heat the vegetable oil in a wok over medium-high heat. Add the ginger and cook until fragrant, 1 to 2 minutes. Add the scallion whites and the lobster meat and cook, tossing, for 20 seconds. Drizzle the cooking wine around the edge of the wok and quickly cover (this helps to lock in flavor). Cook for 2 minutes.

Remove the lid and add the soy sauce mixture and scallion greens and cook for 1 additional minute, stirring constantly. Remove from the heat.

Fill each bao bun with a small amount of the lobster mixture and garnish the lobster mixture with the chives. Fold the buns, then top each bun with chili crisp, if desired.

Mac & Cheese Fritters

TOWN BAR, EDGARTOWN

Martha's Vineyard is a sports town. Not surprising when Boston is just a ferry hop and then some away. The place to watch a game is Town, with its central bar and cool retro decor. Whip up a batch of their bestselling bar snack at home: crispy on the outside and ooey and gooey on the inside (thanks, Velveeta), these fritters are a game-day favorite. The recipe scales up or down, but these fritters disappear fast, so make sure you have enough to go around. Serve with a spicy sauce, like sriracha aioli.

MAKES TWENTY-FOUR (3-INCH) FRITTERS

1 pound Velveeta, cubed

1¼ cups heavy cream

6 tablespoons unsalted butter

3 cloves garlic, minced

Kosher salt and freshly ground black pepper

10 ounces dried small pasta shells

1 cup all-purpose flour, plus more as needed

2 large eggs, beaten

1½ cups panko breadcrumbs

3 cups neutral oil for frying

Place the Velveeta, cream, butter, and garlic in a large skillet over medium-low heat. Cook, stirring frequently with a wooden spoon, until the cheese and butter have melted. Season with salt and pepper.

Meanwhile, bring a large pot of salted water to a boil and cook the pasta until soft, about 8 minutes. Drain. Transfer the pasta to a large baking sheet. Pour the cheese sauce over the pasta and mix thoroughly with a silicone spatula until evenly combined. Taste and adjust seasoning. Chill in the refrigerator until firm, at least 4 hours or overnight.

Line a large baking sheet with parchment paper. Place 3 shallow dishes side by side, one with the flour, one with the beaten eggs, and the last with the panko. Using a cookie scoop, pull off a golf ball–size portion of mac and cheese and roll into a ball. Dredge in the flour, then shake off any excess. Dredge in the egg, then the panko. Set on the prepared baking sheet. Repeat with remaining mac and cheese. Refrigerate the fritters for 30 minutes so they hold their shape when frying.

Line a baking sheet or platter with paper towels. In a heavy pot with high sides or a deep fryer, bring the oil to 350°F to 365°F (a cube of bread dropped in the oil turns golden brown in about 15 seconds). Fry the balls in batches until golden brown, 3 to 5 minutes, turning occasionally so they fry evenly on all sides. Drain on the paper towels, and serve hot.

Martha's Vineyard Ceviche

TIGERHAWK, OAK BLUFFS

This colorful ceviche is a twist on traditional ceviche, enjoyed throughout Peru, the home country of TigerHawk owner and chef Jimmy Alvarado. "Peru and Martha's Vineyard have a lot in common," says Jimmy. "Both are very coastal and share some of the same seafood." Jimmy turns to ceviche for a game-day snack or to cure a hangover. Much like the rest of TigerHawk's menu of inventive bowls and bites (including the very popular fried chicken sandwiches), this ceviche packs a punch: the textures, freshness, spice, and hint of sweetness come together to create a knockout of a dish. The recipe for the zesty leche de tigre, or tiger's milk, used in the dish was handed down to Jimmy by his grandfather, who owned a cevicheria in Lima. "It's the best I've ever had; I could take shots of it," he says. Don't sleep on the crunchy, salty accompaniment of cancha (shallow-fried chulpe corn kernels)—a popular Peruvian bar snack that is utterly addictive. Chulpe corn gets toasty but does not puff like popcorn. It can be found online or at specialty retailers.

SERVES 4

1 tablespoon vegetable oil

1 cup chulpe corn

1½ teaspoons plus pinch fine sea salt

8 ounces fluke fillet, skinned

8 ounces bay scallops

1 rib celery or 1 celery heart, chopped

2 small cloves garlic

1 (¼-inch) piece ginger, peeled

1 cup fresh lime juice (from about 8 limes)

2 teaspoons hot sauce, such as TigerHawk pineapple-habanero hot sauce, or to taste

1 tablespoon kosher salt

1 large red onion, thinly sliced

8 littleneck clams, cleaned

¾ cup cilantro leaves

1 medium sweet potato, cooked, peeled, and pureed smooth

Microgreens for garnish

For the cancha, heat the vegetable oil in a large skillet over medium heat. Once the oil is shimmering, add the corn and fry, shaking the pan frequently, until the kernels start to pop, 2 to 3 minutes.

Cover the skillet, reduce the heat to medium-low, and cook, continuing to shake the pan frequently, until the corn is a deep golden brown, about 5 minutes.

Transfer the corn to a bowl, sprinkle with 1 teaspoon sea salt, and cool to room temperature. Store in an airtight container for up to 2 weeks.

Slice the fluke into 1¼ by ¾-inch strips. Set aside 2 tablespoons of trimmings. Place the strips in a bowl, cover, and refrigerate.

To make the leche de tigre, combine the fish trimmings, 8 bay scallops, celery, garlic, ginger, and lime juice in a food processor fitted with the metal blade or in a blender and allow to sit at room temperature for 5 minutes. Process the mixture until very smooth. Strain the mixture through a fine-mesh sieve into a medium bowl. Stir in the hot sauce and the remaining ½ teaspoon sea salt. Refrigerate, covered, for up to 2 hours.

Place the remaining scallops in a medium bowl. Combine the kosher salt with 2 cups water and whisk until dissolved. Pour this over the scallops, cover, and refrigerate for 30 minutes.

Soak the onion in ice water for 10 minutes. Drain and pat dry with paper towels, then return to the bowl and refrigerate, covered, until ready to use.

Combine the clams and 3 tablespoons water in a medium saucepan and place over medium heat. Cover and steam until the clams open, about 3 minutes. Transfer to a bowl, discarding any clams that don't open.

Place the fluke strips in a medium bowl and sprinkle with a pinch of fine sea salt. After 2 minutes, drain the scallops and add to the bowl with the clams. Add the leche de tigre, toss to combine, and allow to rest at room temperature for 2 minutes. Add the onion and cilantro and mix gently with a spoon. Divide the ceviche among individual plates and sprinkle with cilantro leaves and the corn. Spoon the sweet potato puree into a piping bag fitted with a round tip and pipe rounds over the ceviche. Garnish with microgreens.

Muhammara with Homemade Pita

CATBOAT COFFEE CO., VINEYARD HAVEN

After years of cooking in New York City, Catboat Coffee Co. co-owner Naji Boustany made the move to Martha's Vineyard, which he found similar to his home city of Beirut. "There is a real sense of community here," he says. The island's farm-to-table cooking is another reminder of Lebanon, where he learned to cook from the women of his family. Nostalgia for Beirut's café culture inspired him to open his coffee shop. "The social life in America revolves around bars and pubs. In Lebanon, the café is where you meet friends and can spend hours with no rush. I wanted to bring that culture here."

He has done just that, curating the shop's offerings to include picnic-inspired specialty items, which are a perfect pairing for the charcuterie boards created by Morgen Schroeder, his cheesemonger sister-in-law. Naji offers freshly made sandwiches, salads, and dips, like the popular muhammara, a zesty roasted red pepper and walnut dip. Try it alongside grilled meats, or simply enjoy scooping it up with warm pita. Stovetop pita tends to be soft; for puffy pockets, bake the flattened dough balls in a 500°F oven for 3 to 5 minutes.

SERVES 4 TO 6

Pita

2 teaspoons sugar

2 tablespoons olive oil

2 teaspoons instant yeast

2⅔ cups all-purpose flour, plus more for work surface

2 teaspoons kosher salt

Muhammara

2 red bell peppers

¼ cup extra virgin olive oil, plus more for pan and drizzling

½ cup walnut halves, plus more for garnish

¾ cup breadcrumbs

1 clove garlic, roughly chopped

2 tablespoons pomegranate molasses

1 teaspoon Aleppo pepper

1 teaspoon sumac

½ teaspoon kosher salt

1 tablespoon lemon juice

1 radish, thinly sliced, for garnish

Mint leaves for garnish

Make the pita: In a large bowl, whisk the sugar with ¾ cup plus 3 tablespoons lukewarm water and the oil in a large bowl. Add the yeast, flour, and salt and stir with a wooden spoon to combine. Knead the dough on a lightly floured surface until smooth and slightly tacky, 8 minutes. Don't add too much flour; it should be tacky. Clean the bowl and return the dough to the bowl. Cover with a kitchen towel and let rest until doubled in size, 45 minutes to 1 hour.

Make the muhammara: Preheat the oven to 425°F. Brush the bell peppers with 1 tablespoon of the olive oil and place on a lightly oiled baking sheet. Roast the peppers for 30 minutes, turning once halfway through. While the peppers are roasting, place the walnuts on a small baking sheet and toast in the oven for 3 to 4 minutes until they smell nutty. Set aside a few walnuts for garnish. Remove the peppers from the oven, cool slightly until easy to handle, then cut the peppers in half and remove the seeds. Slice the peppers thinly.

In a food processor fitted with the metal blade, combine the roasted red pepper strips with the remaining 3 tablespoons olive oil, the walnuts, breadcrumbs, garlic, pomegranate molasses, Aleppo pepper, sumac, and salt. Blend to a smooth paste, then add the lemon juice and process a few seconds more.

Transfer to a serving bowl, drizzle with more olive oil, and garnish with the walnuts, radish, and mint.

To continue with the pita, divide the dough into 6 even portions, shape into balls, and place on a work surface. Cover with a kitchen towel and rest on the counter for 20 minutes.

Lightly flour the work surface. Flatten a ball of dough with the palm of your hand. Gently roll out to a 6- to 7-inch diameter. If you find that the dough stretches back when rolling, let it rest a few minutes longer. Toss the round from hand to hand to shake off excess flour. Set aside, covered with a kitchen towel, and repeat with remaining dough balls.

Heat a large, cast-iron skillet over medium-high heat for 5 minutes. Place 1 dough round on the skillet and cook until bubbles form, about 30 seconds, then turn and cook for 30 additional seconds. Turn the bread again and cook for 10 seconds. Remove to a plate and keep warm while you repeat with remaining breads. Serve warm with the dip.

Oysters
with Watermelon-Jalapeño Mignonette

SIGNATURE OYSTER FARM, EDGARTOWN

A salt bomb with an amazing sweet-as-candy finish. Hard to beat that for a flavor profile for oysters. "The description fits. They're really good," smiles Signature Oyster Farm owner Ryan Smith, whose exquisite oysters are enjoyed at island restaurants and across the country. Cultivating oysters is intense work, seven-days-a-week work, but Ryan loves what he does. He's joined by his wife, Julia, the only female oyster farm owner on the island. They've perfected a uniquely sustainable method that tumbles the oysters, not only to deliver a clean shell with polished edges but to develop deeper cups, resulting in plumper meat. This is their signature mignonette, served on the oyster tours they run throughout the summer. Even if you're a purist and your go-to is the naked oyster, this pretty-in-pink mignonette complements the finest bivalves.

MAKES ¼ CUP, ENOUGH TO ACCOMPANY 12 OYSTERS

1 tablespoon finely minced shallot

2 tablespoons rice vinegar

½ teaspoon local honey

1 slice seeded jalapeño (or keep the seeds if you want a kick)

1 (1-inch) cube seedless watermelon, rind removed

Kosher salt and freshly ground black pepper

12 oysters, preferably Signature Oysters

In a small food processor, combine the shallot, vinegar, honey, jalapeño, watermelon, and 2 teaspoons water. Pulse to combine. Transfer to a small bowl and season lightly with salt and pepper.

Shuck the oysters and place on an oyster tray filled with ice. Spoon some of the mignonette on the oysters before slurping.

Pâté for a Party

Charcuterie is one of Tyler Potter's great loves, and he wants more people to try making it. "Having a back-pocket recipe for charcuterie makes you pretty badass," says Tyler, owner of The Swimming Pig. "Sure, pâté, like this coarser-style pâté de campagne, can be intimidating. But, when you break it down it's a (mostly) pork meatloaf poached in a water bath. Anyone can make this."

The most important step in making a proper pâté is sourcing quality meats. On Martha's Vineyard, Tyler chooses The Grey Barn, but seek out your local butcher. If you don't have a meat grinder or grinder attachment for a stand mixer, ask your butcher to grind the pork and bacon.

Pâté de campagne can be crafted to your personal tastes. Replace the raisins with cranberries, or switch out the Madeira for any sweet dessert booze like brandy or sherry.

This luxurious treat will take you from summer soirée to fall weekend cuddled up by the fire with a sleeve of crackers and a bottle of red.

MAKES 1 TERRINE; SERVES 8 TO 10

1 pound 14 ounces pork shoulder

13 ounces bacon

4½ ounces chicken livers, cleaned and roughly chopped

2 tablespoons kosher salt

2¼ teaspoons coarsely ground black pepper

¾ teaspoon granulated garlic

¾ teaspoon ground coriander

¼ teaspoon ground cloves

¼ teaspoon ground cinnamon

¼ teaspoon ground nutmeg

¼ teaspoon ground cayenne pepper

2 teaspoons dried thyme

4 large eggs

¾ cup shelled pistachios

⅓ cup golden raisins

¼ cup Madeira

Finely minced flat-leaf parsley leaves for garnish

Cornichons, whole grain mustard, and crackers for serving

Position an oven rack in the center of the oven and preheat to 300°F.

If grinding the meat yourself, cut the pork and bacon into cubes small enough to fit into the grinder. Freeze for 10 minutes. Use a medium grinding plate and grind the meat. Transfer to the bowl of a stand mixer fitted with the paddle attachment.

To the bowl add the chicken livers, seasonings, eggs, pistachios, raisins, and Madeira. Combine on medium-high speed until the mixture starts to pull away from the sides of the bowl, about 5 minutes. You can also do this by hand, mixing vigorously with a wooden spoon until the mixture is fully incorporated.

Completely fill a 9 by 5–inch loaf pan with the mixture, using the back of your hand to pack it in as tightly as possible. Tap it assertively on the counter over a towel to remove any air pockets. Wrap the top of the loaf pan tightly with foil and seal the edges well. Place the loaf pan in a deep roasting pan and fill with warm water until the water almost reaches the brim of the loaf pan. Cover the loaf pan and roasting pan with another layer of foil. Roast for 1½ hours. Carefully remove from the oven (the pan is full of very hot water). Remove the foil covering the roasting pan. Let the foil-covered loaf pan cool in the water bath for 1 hour.

Remove the loaf pan from the water bath and refrigerate, still covered with the foil. Place something heavy, such as cans or jars, on top of the foil to press the pâté down evenly. Refrigerate for at least 8 hours.

The next day, run an offset spatula around the edge of the pan and unmold the pâté onto a serving platter. Serve with cornichons, mustard, and crackers. Wrap any leftover pâté tightly in plastic wrap and refrigerate for up to 1 week.

Roast Clams
with Hot Sauce Butter

MIMI'S HITTIN' THE SAUCE, WEST TISBURY

The accidental hot sauce champions. What started back in 2016 as a way to use up a surplus of garden tomatoes (a common conundrum for many Vineyarders), soon became an award-winning line of hot sauces, putting our tiny island on the international hot sauce map. Mimi's Hittin' the Sauce is lovingly made by Cathy and Mark Peters. Mark grows an assortment of peppers in their West Tisbury garden, including some of the world's spiciest, Carolina Reaper and Dragon's Breath, while Cathy is busy cooking, bottling, and shipping their sauces to devotees as far away as Japan and Australia. Their farmers market stand proudly displays awards for their mild to extra-extra hot varieties. "Every time I think we've made the hottest sauce possible, our fans ask for more Scovilles!" laughs Cathy. The small-batch sauces balance heat with flavor, from fruity to smoky, and Cathy recommends adding a shake to everything from chowder to eggs, stuffed clams, and, yes, chicken wings (which she likes to parboil in hot sauce water for extra flavor). Try this easy butter on roast clams or oysters; the flames lightly caramelize the buttery juices, making the bivalves extra slurpable. The butter is also delicious on grilled shrimp and corn.

SERVES 4

4 tablespoons unsalted butter, softened

1 teaspoon hot sauce, such as Mimi's Hittin' the Sauce

12 littleneck clams

Lemon wedges for serving

Use a wooden spoon to combine the butter and hot sauce in a small bowl.

Heat a grill to high. Place the clams on the grate. They will open in 3 to 5 minutes. Carefully remove with tongs—they're very hot!—and set on a platter. Wearing oven mitts, remove the top shells. Dot each clam with 1 teaspoon of hot sauce butter, then return to the grill until the butter melts and slightly caramelizes, 1 to 2 minutes. Carefully remove with tongs, squeeze lemon over the top, and enjoy.

No grill? No problem! Preheat the oven to 400°F. Place the clams on a small baking sheet and roast until they open, 8 to 12 minutes. Proceed as above, roasting the clams with the hot sauce butter in the oven for 3 minutes.

Scallop Crudo
with Horseradish Crema

19 RAW OYSTER BAR, EDGARTOWN

When chef and owner Joe Monteiro and his fourth-generation Vineyarder wife, Emily, opened 19 Raw Oyster Bar in 2017, the restaurant enticed diners with its seafood-forward menu, welcoming atmosphere, and hospitality. "Having access to incredibly fresh seafood from the waters of New England is so valuable," Joe explains. Joe's scallop crudo is a guest favorite, a sweet and subtly smoky appetizer fragrant with Japanese aromatics. "In less than thirty-six hours my supplier, The Net Result, gets live scallops from the ocean floor to my door," he says. The crudo pairs perfectly with a Wash Ashore beer, and for good reason: Joe and a few friends cofounded the island-born company featuring organically brewed beer. "The sense of community here is unparalleled, and I feel grateful to be a part of it."

SERVES 2

Horseradish Crema

- ½ cup full-fat sour cream
- ¼ cup best-quality mayonnaise
- ¼ cup grated fresh horseradish
- 1½ teaspoons whole-grain mustard
- ½ teaspoon kosher salt
- ½ teaspoon freshly ground black pepper

Scallop Crudo

- 2 large sea scallops (about 2½ inches in diameter)
- 1 (2-inch) piece ginger, peeled and cut into matchsticks
- 2 tablespoons sliced scallions
- 2 tablespoons ponzu
- 2 tablespoons sesame oil

Make the horseradish crema: Combine the sour cream, mayonnaise, horseradish, mustard, salt, and pepper in a small bowl. Refrigerate for at least 30 minutes and up to 1 hour. (You will only need 2 tablespoons of this mixture, but the remainder can be stored in the refrigerator in an airtight container for up to 2 weeks; try it over grilled fish or steak.)

Make the scallop crudo: Spread 2 tablespoons of the chilled crema on a plate. Slice the scallops with a very sharp knife into very thin discs and arrange over the crema, overlapping slightly. Sprinkle the ginger and scallions over the scallops. Drizzle the ponzu over the scallops.

Heat the sesame oil in a small saucepan until smoking. Drizzle the oil over the scallops and serve immediately.

Striper Ceviche
with Kombucha

KULTURE CLUB MV, VINEYARD HAVEN

Nina Gordon brews artisanal, small-batch raw kombucha (a sparkling, fermented tea) with flavors inspired by her surroundings. Cranberries and blueberries, foraged elderberries and sassafras root—the island is her muse. The lightly tart drink is low in sugar but loaded with live probiotic cultures, and like other fermented foods (think kimchi and yogurt), it's great for gut health, digestion, and improving immunity. "Kombucha is so versatile," says Nina, smiling. "I add it to smoothies. You can make cocktails with it. I've even brined chicken with it before frying." Out fishing with a friend one day, Nina caught a beautiful striped bass and she then had enough fish to try several different dishes. Since ceviche needs an acid like lemon or vinegar to "cook" the fish, and is often flavored with ginger, she turned to her lemon-ginger turmeric "booch." The recipe was an epiphany.

Stripers are a prized local fish (celebrated with an annual derby started in 1946) with a slightly sweet flavor and translucent light pink flesh that turns opaque white when cooked. If striper is not available, substitute with other firm white fish like black sea bass, fluke, or flounder.

SERVES 4

1 pound striped bass fillet, skinned and cut into cubes

½ cup lemon-ginger kombucha, such as Kulture Club MV lemon, ginger, and turmeric kombucha

2 small ripe tomatoes, diced

¼ red onion, finely diced

1 jalapeño, seeded and minced

1 teaspoon kosher salt, plus more if needed

½ cup chopped cilantro leaves

2 tablespoons fresh lime juice

Lime wedges for serving

Tortilla chips for serving

Toss together the fish, kombucha, tomatoes, onion, jalapeño, and salt in a medium bowl. Cover with a lid and refrigerate until the fish turns opaque, 10 to 15 minutes.

Add the cilantro and lime juice and gently toss, then taste for seasoning; add more salt, if necessary. Serve with lime wedges and tortilla chips.

Stuffed Quahogs

THE NET RESULT, VINEYARD HAVEN

Part fish market, part takeout, The Net Result has been guided by its dedication to fresh seafood since opening in 1985. In the summer, crowds fill the outdoor picnic tables with platters of steamed lobster, fried clams, and the perfect fish sandwich. Thankfully, The Net Result is open year-round, bringing in the first of the tautog (blackfish) in September, sweet bay scallops in November, and offering oysters, shrimp cocktail, and crab cakes for holiday festivities. General manager Mike Holtham's stuffies, or stuffed quahogs, are justifiably famous. Quahogs (pronounced *ko-hogs*) have pearlescent purple shells that the Wampanoag used as currency, and that still feature in beautiful jewelry made by the tribe. Those same shells make a clever serving vessel. Rich and savory, stuffed clams make a crowd-pleasing appetizer at parties and potlucks, whether served on their own or with cocktail sauce. You can use cherrystone clams if quahogs are not available.

SERVES 10

10 large quahog clams, cleaned

3 tablespoons unsalted butter

½ cup finely diced white onion

2 cloves garlic, minced

½ cup finely diced green bell pepper

½ cup finely diced red bell pepper

½ teaspoon crushed red pepper flakes

5 slices plain white bread, cut into 1-inch squares

1¾ cups Italian seasoned coarse breadcrumbs

1 tablespoon sweet paprika

Bring 2 inches of water to a boil in a large pot over medium-high heat. Add the clams and cover with a lid. Steam the clams until fully open, 5 to 7 minutes after the water returns to a boil. Remove the clams with a slotted spoon and place in a colander to drain. Strain the liquid through a fine-mesh strainer into a bowl and reserve.

Once the clams are cool enough to handle, remove the clam meat from the shells, reserving the shells, and mince the meat. Break each clam shell at the hinge to make two pieces.

Melt 2 tablespoons of the butter in a medium saucepan over medium-low heat. Add the onion and garlic and cook, stirring frequently, until slightly softened, 3 to 4 minutes. Add the bell peppers and cook until tender, stirring occasionally, about 10 minutes. Add the red pepper flakes and stir to combine, then add ½ cup of the reserved clam cooking liquid and the chopped clams.

Combine the white bread and Italian breadcrumbs in a large bowl with a large spoon. Add the vegetable-clam mixture and stir to combine. If the mix seems too dry, add more of the clam juice 1 tablespoon at a time; the ingredients should hold together. Allow the mixture to cool slightly.

Preheat the oven to 425°F. Pack about ⅓ cup of the mixture into each clam shell and place the shells on a baking sheet. Melt the remaining 1 tablespoon butter and drizzle it over the clams. Dust with the paprika.

Bake the clams until golden brown, 12 to 15 minutes. Serve hot.

Swordfish Gravlax

MENEMSHA FISH MARKET, CHILMARK

While you're waiting to order a cup of award-winning chowder at Menemsha Fish Market, ponder this moment in local history: back in the 1970s, owner Stan Larsen hooked a 1,000-pound swordfish, not too far off in size from Jay Lagemann's iconic *Swordfish Harpooner* sculpture a few steps away on Menemsha Beach. Stan is certainly impressive, yet warmly welcoming to those who travel near and far for his fresh catch. While the fishing industry deals with climate change and overfishing, Stan is committed to supporting sustainable fishing, and challenges our reliance on energy. "Look for seafood recipes that use less energy, like ceviche or gravlax," suggests Stan. On a recent visit, I sampled Stan's homemade salmon gravlax. When I spotted some spanking fresh swordfish—Stan's favorite—behind the counter, it sparked an idea. How about swordfish gravlax? We applied Stan's classic gravlax recipe and a star was born.

MAKES 1 POUND GRAVLAX; SERVES 6 TO 8

½ cup Himalayan pink salt

½ cup brown sugar

1 pound swordfish steaks, about 1 inch thick

½ cup dill fronds, roughly chopped

Dill, bagels, cream cheese, sliced red onion, and sliced tomato for serving

Mix the salt and sugar in a small bowl and spread half the mix evenly on the bottom of a glass dish large enough to hold the fish in a single layer. Arrange the swordfish on top. Sprinkle the rest of the salt and sugar on top of the swordfish. Press the chopped dill onto the surface. Cover and refrigerate for 12 hours.

After 12 hours, flip the fish, and continue curing in the refrigerator for another 24 to 36 hours. (Taste after 24 hours and continue curing to your taste.) Cut a thin slice to test the seasoning. If it's too salty, run both sides of the fish under cold tap water and pat dry with paper towels.

Slice the fish thinly and arrange on a platter with dill. Serve with bagels, cream cheese, onion, and tomato, for a delicious twist on bagels and lox.

Captain Buddy Vanderhoop

Some folks put their hearts on their sleeves when they fall in love. Captain Buddy Vanderhoop went one step further when he began courting his wife, Lisa. "I handed her a beating tuna heart, and that was it," laughs Buddy.

A fishing charter captain for over thirty-five years, Buddy is a member of the Wampanoag Tribe of Aquinnah, and the eldest of the Vanderhoop siblings (sister Juli is the owner of Orange Peel Bakery). His childhood was spent clamming and foraging for beach plums, cranberries, and hazelnuts—a passion that continues to this day. During the summer and fall, he takes guests out on his Tomahawk fishing charter, which over the years has welcomed a bevy of famous guests. Few people know our waters like Buddy, who comes from a long line of fishermen dating back to the whaling days. He met Lisa, an acclaimed photographer and producer who traveled the world filming science and nature documentaries, on Cape Cod and they married in 1995. They live in Aquinnah.

Lisa: After such a busy summer, we really look forward to the off-season. Our perfect day starts by taking our Weimaraner, Willie, for long walks on the empty beaches. Fall and winter are such beautiful seasons on the island. The colors, the quiet. It's a restorative time.

Buddy: We will hunt, fish, and scallop. The best mussels are right there [motioning to Menemsha Basin]. Then we'll come home and cook up a feast. Would you like a recipe for bluefin tuna? Marinate tuna steaks in honey, soy sauce, and toasted sesame oil for 2 to 3 hours, then coat in toasted sesame seeds. Sear in a lightly oiled skillet over medium-high heat for 1 minute on each side. The flavor is sensational and you get a nice crunch on the outside.

Or how about venison? Take the backstrap—that's the best part—and marinate in beach plum jelly,

sesame oil, soy sauce, garlic, rosemary, thyme, and Chambord liqueur. Marinate in the refrigerator for 12 to 24 hours, then grill for 4 to 5 minutes per side and allow to rest for 10 minutes. It's sweet and sour and so good.

In the evening, we prefer to stay in and have a quiet night at home. Why go out when we can make a five-star meal at home?

Sides & Vegetables

Basil & Feta Summer Squash Stew

GHOST ISLAND FARM, WEST TISBURY

You can't visit Ghost Island Farm without being surprised and delighted. Robots, aliens, and "the girls" (a gang of mannequins dotted around the farm) welcome you as you pull up. At Halloween, weird and wonderful creations, complete with smoke machines and light displays, enchant curious passersby. The fantastical farm operated by Rusty Gordon and Sarah Crittenden has been serving the community since 2012, and it is dedicated to growing high-quality produce without chemical sprays or plastic coverings. Just a lot of hard work by good people. "We have a happy team here," smiles Rusty. "You want to spend your day with people you like." The farm's year-round CSA is a little different from most in that it allows members to choose exactly what they like, when they like. Don't pass up their homemade garlic and chili powders, which pack a real punch. Rusty grows dozens of varieties of tomatoes, his favorite crop, to the delight of tomato-mad Vineyarders. This restorative vegetable stew, made with the farm's famous tomatoes, instantly nourishes, and is hearty enough to stand on its own as a main course with good bread.

SERVES 4 TO 6

8 ounces feta, broken into chunks

4 large shiitake mushrooms, stemmed and sliced

3 medium tomatoes, roughly chopped

3 medium summer squash, sliced into ½-inch-thick half-moons

1 large green bell pepper, seeded and coarsely chopped

1 small yellow onion, coarsely chopped

¾ cup loosely packed basil leaves

1 tablespoon sugar

1 tablespoon vegetable oil

½ teaspoon kosher salt

½ teaspoon freshly ground black pepper

¼ teaspoon garlic powder

Preheat the oven to 425°F. Set aside a small amount of the feta. In a 9 by 13–inch baking dish or casserole, toss together the remaining feta, mushrooms, tomatoes, squash, bell pepper, onion, basil, sugar, oil, salt, black pepper, and garlic powder. Tightly cover with foil and bake until the vegetables are crisp-tender, about 45 minutes. Divide among individual soup bowls and top with the reserved feta.

Charred Cucumbers, Shishito Peppers, Garden Herb Oil, Summer Onions & Fromage Blanc

SLIP AWAY FARM, EDGARTOWN

Lily Walter started pretty Slip Away Farm on Chappaquiddick in 2012. Opening a farm anywhere is a challenge, let alone on a remote, salt marsh–covered island with soft, sandy soil. However, with a lot of hard work and the support of a community rooting for her success, the land has blossomed into a beloved flower and vegetable farm. The summer season culminates with a farm dinner helmed by chef Molly Levine, who splits her time between Martha's Vineyard, New York's Hudson Valley, and the West Coast.

This is a story of collaboration, of two female business owners creating magic in tribute to the land they so love. "We met in 2016 when I was running Behind the Bookstore" explains Molly. "Collins Heavener, who worked with Lily, would bring fresh vegetables on the bike wagon over the Chappy ferry to the restaurant." Instead of writing a menu and then sourcing ingredients, Molly prefers to build a meal around the produce. "Here are these things, how can we make them work together?" she asks herself. "The produce is so beautiful, so nutrient-dense, that it only needs a light hand to bring it together." It's a liberating way for all of us to cook.

Soon after, the idea to partner on an annual farm dinner, celebrating food, farming, and community, was born. How do they plan these experiences? "I say to Molly, 'This is what we have in the field this week, do what you do best!'" says Lily. "And now Collins and his wife, Lucy Leopold, produce chicken and lamb on nearby Marshall Farm," beams Molly. "It's incredible to have the entire meal come from Chappy." Lily agrees, "The farm's diversity is showcased in each course."

These events are the highlight of the summer for Lily and Molly. "There's such a nice energy at these dinners. You're eating good food from the place it was grown—a true Vineyard experience."

Molly's Westerly Canteen, a restaurant housed in an Airstream in the Hudson Valley, was born from these dinners, with the same ethos for sourcing hyper-locally, cooking with intention, and creating memorable experiences. Molly smiles, "Slip Away Farm is a place of joy, my home away from home."

SERVES 4

Herb Oil

Leaves of 1 bunch basil (reserve a few leaves for garnish)

1 bunch flat-leaf parsley, stems and leaves roughly chopped

2 large cloves garlic

1 teaspoon green peppercorns (if you don't have green, black works too)

Kosher salt

1½ cups extra virgin olive oil

Juice of 1 small lemon

2 teaspoons champagne vinegar

Cucumbers and Shishitos

4 to 6 cucumbers (see Note, page 112), cut into 4- to 6-inch-long, 1-inch-wide spears

8 ounces shishito peppers

½ cup grapeseed oil

Kosher salt

2 white summer onions, thinly shaved on a mandoline

½ cup fromage blanc, such as Mermaid Farm

RECIPE CONTINUES

Make the herb oil: Prepare a bowl of ice water and bring a small saucepan of water to a boil. Add the basil leaves to the boiling water and boil for 10 seconds. Remove with a slotted spoon and transfer to the ice water. Drain the leaves, spread on kitchen towels, and gently press out as much water as possible. Place the basil and parsley in a blender with the garlic, peppercorns, and a good pinch of salt. Blend on medium-high speed while adding the olive oil in a thin stream. Add the lemon juice and vinegar. Taste and adjust for salt and acidity. The herb oil should taste somewhat acidic, verging on a salad dressing.

Make the cucumbers and shishitos: Heat a grill to high. Place the cucumbers and shishito peppers on a tray and toss with grapeseed oil to coat. Season generously with salt. Add a few spears of cucumber to the grill, cut sides down. Sear just until there are grill marks, 20 to 30 seconds. Flip until the other cut sides have grill marks. Remove to a tray. Repeat with remaining spears. Place the shishito peppers in a corner of the hot grill. Flip them as they start to blister. Once they are well blistered and puffed, remove them and place them on the tray with the grilled cucumbers.

Generously coat the bottom of a shallow bowl or a serving platter with a lip with herb oil (you may not need all of it—leftovers will keep refrigerated for up to 3 days). Arrange the grilled cucumbers and shishito peppers on top. Scatter the onions and dollop with the fromage blanc. Garnish with basil leaves.

Note: Slip Away Farm grows amazing cucumbers. Any style of slicing cucumber will work for this recipe. Armenian and Japanese-style cucumbers are ideal for grilling as they have less water/seed content than a classic slicer. However, those work great too!

Noli Taylor

Noli Taylor is the executive director of programs and outreach at Island Grown Initiative, where she's worked for almost twenty years. She lives in Aquinnah with her husband, Isaac, their children, Emmett and Tillie, and her parents. Isaac grew up across the street from where they live now, and his parents, sister, aunts, and uncles continue to live nearby.

My perfect day would be a Saturday in late September when it's not so crowded or busy as during the summer, but the weather is lovely and the water is still warm. We like to get up early and take our dog to Philbin Beach. After that, we might have breakfast at Isaac's family's restaurant, the Outermost Inn, and head to West Basin. We take the bike ferry across to Menemsha, where we have a boat. We love to be out on the water, so we'd anchor and swim near the Aquinnah cliffs. Isaac and the kids would fish, and I'd read a book. Bliss!

When we get back to the dock, there's always time for ice cream at Menemsha Galley, before hopping on the bike ferry back to Aquinnah. At home, in the late afternoon sun, we pick veggies from our garden and make a nice supper to share with my parents, friends, and neighbors. The fact that my children get to grow up in a place with deep family roots, as the seventeenth generation to be born on this island, means so much to me.

It's very special that we get to live in a place so rich with cultural history, among members of the Wampanoag Tribe whose ancestors have continuously been on this land for over twelve thousand years. And I love living on an island with no chain stores, no billboards, no outside corporate influence. People who live here still know how to fish and farm and fix things when they break, and make and build and cook things. After growing up on the West Coast and seeing rampant development swallowing up sacred places, I feel so thankful to be part of a community that is as cautious and caring as this one is.

Fall Root Vegetable Gratin

ISLAND GROWN INITIATIVE, VINEYARD HAVEN

While Martha's Vineyard may dazzle with celebrity visitors, waterfront properties, and mega yachts, that is not the full picture of the island. Food insecurity has skyrocketed in recent years, and today, 20 percent of the population turns to the food pantry run by Island Grown Initiative (IGI) at some point during the year.

IGI is a bastion of the community, running grassroots programs that support the island's food needs. Farm-to-school programs and edible gardens provide hands-on experience for all students on how to grow and cook healthy food. Tens of thousands of meals are provided through the pantry and for free during school vacations. The project's forty-acre regenerative farm grows food for all these programs, and anyone can sign up to glean, helping to reduce food waste. "We work with our partners in the farming community to learn about ways to grow foods that are climate resilient and climate supportive; we work with fishing and aquaculture partners to try and find ways to keep more of their catch on island rather than being exported; and we're working with regional food producers and distributors to bring more northeastern-grown food to the island," says Noli Taylor, Executive Director of Programs and Outreach. "Shortening the food supply chain to get more of the food we eat to come from as close to home as possible is important for long-term food stability." CSA memberships subsidize donations to the pantry. IGI food consultant and chef Naji Boustany knows a CSA box in February might not be as inspiring as one in July, so he came up with this fall gratin that makes root vegetables—yes, even parsnips!—the stars. It's a sublime meat-free lunch or side dish that will disappear fast at an autumnal potluck.

SERVES 4 TO 6

1 tablespoon unsalted butter, softened

4 small beets, trimmed

2 large parsnips, trimmed

2 carrots

1 large sweet potato

¾ cup heavy cream

4 teaspoons minced thyme leaves

⅓ cup grated Parmesan

Kosher salt and freshly ground black pepper

1 clove garlic, minced

⅓ cup shredded cheddar

⅓ cup shredded Gruyère

⅓ cup shredded mozzarella

Flat-leaf parsley leaves for garnish

Preheat the oven to 400°F. Coat a 9-inch cast-iron skillet with the butter.

Slice the beets, parsnips, carrots, and sweet potato into very thin rounds (using a mandoline is best) and transfer each vegetable to its own small bowl. Add 2 tablespoons cream, 1 teaspoon thyme, and 1 tablespoon Parmesan to each vegetable. Season each generously with salt and pepper. Toss to coat.

Pour the remaining cream into the prepared baking dish and sprinkle with 1 tablespoon Parmesan and the garlic. Stand the vegetable slices vertically around the perimeter of the baking dish, alternating them. Continue to make concentric circles until all the vegetables have been used.

Season the top of the gratin with salt, pepper, and sprinkle with the remaining Parmesan. Cover with foil and bake until the vegetables are soft, about 30 minutes.

Uncover the gratin and top with the cheddar, Gruyère, and mozzarella. Bake, uncovered, for an additional 15 minutes, until the cheese melts and is lightly browned. Garnish with parsley and serve immediately.

Farro Salad
with Cherry Tomatoes, Spinach & Pesto

MILKWEED FARM, CHILMARK

It takes a village. Mallory Watts credits the food and farming community on Martha's Vineyard for supporting her fruit and vegetable farm, which today supplies many of the island's top restaurants and private chefs. In just a few years, Mallory has transformed the 200-year-old Chilmark property into a no-till, chemical-free farm focused on native plants and biodiversity. Hedges of pawpaw, beach plum, American hazelnuts, and fragrant spicebush watch over her prized crops. There's a lot of trial and error and teamwork. "I value collaboration over competition," says Mallory. "I learn so much from the people and places around me. The Allens of Allen Farm, The Grey Barn—they are all stewards of the land, and I'm honored to join them as a farmer on Martha's Vineyard."

This colorful summer side dish adapted from a recipe by Yasmin Fahr in the *New York Times* is one of Mallory's favorites, made with Milkweed's homegrown tomatoes, spinach, purplette onions, and parsley, plus local pesto. It's great with grilled sausages or fish.

SERVES 4

Kosher salt

1 cup farro, rinsed, such as Anson Mills

2 pints cherry or Sungold tomatoes

2 purplette onions, or 1 medium red onion, cut into wedges

3 tablespoons extra virgin olive oil

Freshly ground black pepper

½ to 1 teaspoon crushed red pepper flakes

¼ cup homemade or store-bought pesto, such as Pam's Pesto

Grated zest and juice of 1 medium lemon

2 packed cups baby spinach

½ cup feta, such as Mermaid Farm

¼ cup flat-leaf parsley leaves

Preheat the oven to 400°F. Bring a medium saucepan of salted water to a boil. Add the farro and stir. Simmer over medium-low heat until tender, about 30 minutes.

While the farro cooks, toss the tomatoes and onion wedges with 2 tablespoons of the olive oil on a baking sheet. Season with salt, pepper, and the red pepper flakes. Roast until the tomatoes collapse, 25 to 30 minutes, then broil for 1 to 2 minutes to char the tomatoes slightly.

When the farro has finished cooking, drain and return to the saucepan. Drizzle with the remaining 1 tablespoon olive oil, add the pesto, and lemon zest and juice, and toss to combine. Add the tomatoes, onions, and all the juices from roasting, then stir in the spinach. Taste and adjust seasoning.

Crumble the feta over the top, garnish with the parsley, and serve hot or warm.

Focaccia with Basil Pesto, Roasted Tomatoes & Kalamata Olives

ORANGE PEEL BAKERY, AQUINNAH

"Everything we need is here. This land is majestic," says Juli Vanderhoop, owner of Orange Peel Bakery, on a quiet morning as she looks out over the brook beside her shop. A few minutes later, a customer pulls up, seeking pie and a chat with Juli. They leave with a huge smile and a bag full of freshly baked treats. This continues all morning, the ebb and flow of visitors who travel to Aquinnah as much for something delicious as for spending a moment in Juli's aura.

Juli is a Wampanoag tribal elder and community builder. She traveled the country and the world as a commercial pilot, educator, and EMT, then returned to seek a deeper connection with her ancestral land. Juli smiles: "I returned home sick, and this land, the energy of this place, healed me." Her father, a Medicine Man, and her mother shared their love of baking with her from a young age, and she opened the bakery in 2006. But anyone who knew Juli realized it was never going to be just a bakery. It was always meant to be the quintessence of community. It revolves around a beautiful French clay oven that Juli built herself. The oven churns out pizzas during the summer, beckoning neighbors and strangers to pull up an Adirondack chair and break bread. At any time of day, the honor-system bakery is stocked with croissants (laminated by hand), scones, cookies, and breads with alluring flavors, like this fragrant focaccia. It's a meal in itself, lush with herby oil, melting cherry tomatoes, and briny olives. This is a fairly sticky dough made with poolish, a preferment that adds flavor and structure. It's easy to make, and a fresh loaf disappears fast.

Cooking is a meditation, which Juli impresses on the bakers she welcomes like family no matter their skill sets. She says, "If one of us isn't feeling it, we drop everything and go for a swim. Or go sit with the sunset. You can't bake if your heart isn't in it. The land and sea heal all."

MAKES ONE (9 BY 13–INCH) LOAF; SERVES 8

5½ cups (1½ pounds) all-purpose flour

2¼ teaspoons (1 envelope) instant yeast

1½ tablespoons kosher salt

Extra virgin olive oil for pan

1 cup homemade or best-quality store-bought pesto

1 cup roasted tomatoes in olive oil

1 cup Kalamata olives, pitted

Flaky sea salt, such as Maldon

Make the poolish 10 to 12 hours before baking: In a large bowl, mix 1¾ cups flour, 1 teaspoon yeast, and 1 cup cold water with a wooden spoon until smooth. Cover with a reusable bowl cover (or plastic wrap) and set aside to rest for 10 to 12 hours. The poolish will look spongy with lots of bubbles.

Add 2 cups lukewarm water and the remaining 1¼ teaspoons yeast to the poolish and gently combine with a silicone spatula. Set aside to rest for 5 minutes.

In a medium bowl, combine the remaining 3¾ cups flour and the kosher salt.

Combine the poolish and flour mixture in the bowl of a stand mixer with the dough hook and knead on medium-high until smooth, about 5 minutes. Cover the bowl with a reusable cover and allow the dough to rise until doubled in size, about 1 hour. Generously coat a 9 by 13–inch baking dish with sides at least 2 inches high with olive oil. Fold the dough by wetting your hands and picking up one side of the dough and gently stretching it up and over the top of the dough. Turn the bowl 90 degrees and repeat until you've done a full rotation. Scoop the dough into the prepared pan and press it out toward the edges with your fingers. Cover and allow to rise until thick and puffy, about 45 minutes.

Preheat the oven to 400°F. Spread the pesto over the dough, leaving a ¾-inch border, being careful not to deflate the dough. Garnish with tomatoes and olives. Dimple the dough with your fingers. Sprinkle with flaky salt. Bake until the edges are golden brown, about 40 minutes. Remove and allow to rest for 10 minutes. Enjoy warm.

Fresh Corn Polenta
with Tomato Jam

BLACK JOY MVY, OAK BLUFFS

"Each summer when I bite into my first piece of island corn," says Chef Ting, founder of Black Joy MVY, "I imagine how many ways I can get that sweet, crunchy taste over and over again. My grandmother did not teach me this recipe, but she certainly would have loved it because my grandfather was a farmer who grew a lot of corn. During picking season she was always looking for new ways to use the abundant crop they were lucky enough to reap."

This recipe beautifully highlights the island's prized summer produce. "The ripe red tomatoes bursting with sunshine, the sweet corn picked hours before eating, the basil that grows as high and strong as a baby dinosaur. If, like me, you cannot wait for that first bite of farmstand corn each summer, this recipe is for you," the chef says, smiling.

Chef Ting hosts retreats for leaders of the African diaspora that are focused on exploring joy through health, wealth, and well-being—and creating this recipe was an act of joy. "I am lucky enough to have a daughter Gabriella, who is also a chef," she shares. "We have spent countless hours creating together in the kitchen, and this tomato jam recipe is her brainchild. Making fresh polenta is a moment of quiet joy. Grab a book, lean comfortably against your counter, and stir." To make a vegan version of this dish, omit the butter, mascarpone, and cheese, and cook the corn for 35 minutes to develop deeper caramelization.

SERVES 6 TO 8

Jam

1 tablespoon extra virgin olive oil

6 roma tomatoes, diced

3 cloves garlic, minced

4 tablespoons balsamic vinegar

½ cup sugar

1 tablespoon kosher salt

2 teaspoons freshly ground black pepper

Leaves of 1 bunch basil, cut into ribbons, plus more for garnish

Polenta

12 ears corn, shucked

4 tablespoons unsalted butter

¼ cup extra virgin olive oil

¼ cup mascarpone

¼ cup shredded Parmigiano Reggiano

2 teaspoons agave syrup, if needed

1 tablespoon plus 1 teaspoon smoked salt (or kosher salt)

Freshly ground black pepper

Make the jam: Heat the olive oil in a medium saucepan over medium heat. Add the tomatoes and cook until soft, about 5 minutes. Add the garlic, 3 tablespoons balsamic vinegar, the sugar, salt, pepper, and about three-quarters of the basil. Cook for 15 minutes, then turn the heat to low and add the remaining 1 tablespoon balsamic. Stir, then add the remaining basil. Remove from the heat, cool to room temperature, then refrigerate until thickened, 20 to 30 minutes.

Make the polenta: Cut the corn kernels off the cob (invert a small bowl inside of a larger bowl; set the tip of the cob on the smaller bowl and slice downward). Then, use the dull side of the knife to scrape the milk from the cob by sliding the knife down the cob. Combine the corn and corn milk in a food processor fitted with the metal blade and puree for 90 seconds until broken down but not perfectly smooth.

Add the butter and olive oil to a large, heavy-bottomed skillet and heat over medium-low. Pour in the corn puree and cook, stirring every minute or so, for 25 minutes. When the color brightens and the corn smells sweet, add the mascarpone and Parmigiano and stir to incorporate. Taste, and if the corn is not very sweet, add the agave syrup. Season with salt and pepper.

Spoon the polenta into a shallow serving bowl, top with tomato jam, and garnish with basil.

Kimchi

MV KIMCHEE, VINEYARD HAVEN

Jeisook Thayer is a powerhouse of a Vineyarder. "When I opened my restaurant, Triple Dragon, in the late seventies to support my young family, I offered sushi, miso soup, and fried squid, except I had to call it calamari because the locals were horrified at the idea of eating squid," laughs Jei. The tiny hole-in-the-wall on Beach Road was essentially a bar with a few seats, where celebrity guests would bring their own chairs, tables, and linens. After closing the beloved restaurant, she decided to bring kimchi to the Vineyard masses (well, as mass as the Vineyard can get), producing small batches with ingredients from her garden.

"Making kimchi is easy," she reassures, while whipping up a batch in minutes. Just remember to remove as much air as possible and store the kimchi in a cool place. Air pockets cause spoilage, so pack the kimchi into jars tightly, weighing it down with something heavy like a clean rock. After a couple of days, it's ready to eat, but it also keeps for months or even years. There are endless variations of kimchi, but Jei's version leaves out the sugar and also omits the traditional fish sauce, making it vegan. It is the ideal recipe for preserving the bounty from your summer garden. A jar of kimchi in your fridge is a gateway to a myriad of meal ideas: fried rice, grilled cheese, a comforting stew with soft tofu. How does Jei enjoy her kimchi? Over rice, of course, and in the summer, wrapped around cubes of tofu for an easy lunch that is refreshing and helps to beat the humidity.

Kimchi is packed with probiotics, healthy bacteria that boost your immunity. "Take a shot of kimchi juice a day to keep the doctor away," recommends Jei. "The world has been preserving and fermenting foods for thousands of years. Kimchi is no different from pickles or sauerkraut, and we can all learn from these ancient ways."

MAKES ONE (16-OUNCE) JAR

1 large napa cabbage

1 heaping tablespoon kosher salt

1 (3- to 4-inch) piece ginger, peeled and minced

3 large cloves garlic, minced

1 bunch scallions, sliced into 1½-inch pieces

¼ cup gochugaru (Korean red pepper flakes)

Slice the cabbage into 2-inch pieces and place in a large bowl. Sprinkle with the salt and let it sit at room temperature for 2 to 3 hours. Drain off the salt water that accumulates in the bottom of the bowl. Add the ginger, garlic, and scallions to the bowl.

Wear food prep gloves to mix in the gochugaru and 1 cup water with your hands. Pack tightly into a clean 16-ounce glass jar with a tight-fitting lid, pressing down firmly to eliminate any air pockets. Pour the juice left in the bowl into the jar. Wrap a clean, heavy rock in plastic wrap and place directly on top of the kimchi to further remove any air pockets. Close the lid on the jar, but not too tightly, and place in a cool spot on your kitchen counter (on a plate, as some liquid can escape).

After 1 day, remove the lid. You should see some bubbles around the edge and surface. If you see bubbles, taste the kimchi. If you're happy with the crunch and flavor, remove the rock, press the kimchi down with a clean spoon, close the lid, and move it to the refrigerator, where the fermentation will slow down. Otherwise, continue to store in a cool part of your kitchen for another day or two for the characteristic sourness to develop before placing in the refrigerator. (Jei keeps her kimchi on the counter for 1 to 3 days before moving it to the refrigerator.) If the cabbage is soft and not crunchy, there may be spoilage because you didn't pack the kimchi tightly enough or did not salt the cabbage enough. Throw away soft kimchi and start again.

Pão de Queijo

SWEET BITES, VINEYARD HAVEN

"My wife, Sonia, and I fell in love with Martha's Vineyard as soon as we arrived in the nineties," says Valerio Destefani, sitting on the patio of their Sweet Bites café. "It has so much in common with our small town in Brazil—a warm, agricultural community. We knew we wouldn't leave." Their year-round café attracts locals as well as visitors, who pop in for sweet and savory bites inspired by their family recipes, like this Brazilian cheese bread. Soft and chewy, these rolls are made with tapioca flour, so they're naturally gluten-free. It's best to use a stand mixer as the dough is hard to mix by hand. Otherwise, they're easy to make, and nothing beats the smell of freshly baked pão.

MAKES 20 ROLLS

1 cup whole milk	2 large eggs, beaten
½ cup vegetable oil	¾ cup shredded Parmesan
1 teaspoon kosher salt	
2 cups tapioca flour	¾ cup shredded mozzarella

Preheat the oven to 350°F. Line a baking sheet with parchment paper.

Combine the milk, oil, and salt in a medium saucepan and bring to a boil over medium heat. Remove from the heat as soon as it comes to a rolling boil. Stir in the tapioca flour until thoroughly incorporated and you see no more dry flour. The dough will be grainy and gelatinous.

Transfer the dough to the bowl of a stand mixer fitted with the paddle attachment. Beat the dough on medium speed until smooth and cool enough that you can hold your finger against the dough for several seconds, about 2 minutes.

With the mixer running, add half of the eggs. When fully incorporated, add the remaining eggs and mix until fully incorporated. Scrape down the sides of the bowl.

With the mixer still on medium, beat in the cheeses until fully incorporated. The resulting dough will be very sticky, stretchy, and soft.

Using a tablespoon measure or ice cream scoop, mound rounded portions of the dough on the prepared baking sheet. (Dip your spoon or scoop into water to prevent sticking.) Space the mounds 1 to 2 inches apart.

Bake until the balls have puffed, the outsides are dry, and they are just starting to color, 25 to 28 minutes. Enjoy warm or at room temperature.

Spring Rolls

WHIPPOORWILL FARM, WEST TISBURY

Rose Willett has a lot on her plate. And that's just the way she likes it. Combining her love of food and farming, she runs North Tisbury Farm and the four-and-a-half-acre Whippoorwill Farm. The regenerative farm supplies the market (and its own darling farmstand) with herbs, vegetables, and flowers, like the edible flowers that gild these (almost) too-pretty-to-eat vegetable rice paper rolls. Beyond beach or boat fare, the rolls make a colorful contribution to a potluck or lunchbox.

MAKES 8 ROLLS; SERVES 4

2 ounces rice vermicelli

1 teaspoon toasted sesame oil

8 rice paper wrappers

1 cup tatsoi leaves, torn

1 cup thinly sliced mustard greens

1 cup thinly sliced napa cabbage

1 cup thinly sliced red cabbage

2 medium carrots, cut into matchsticks

2 scallions, cut into matchsticks

1 daikon radish, cut into matchsticks

1 cucumber, seeded and thinly sliced

1 red bell pepper, seeded and thinly sliced

¼ cup fresh cilantro leaves

¼ cup fresh mint leaves

Edible flowers for finishing

Peanut Sauce for serving (recipe follows)

Nuoc Cham for serving (recipe follows)

Soy-Ginger Sesame Sauce for serving (recipe follows)

Cook the rice vermicelli according to the package instructions. Drain, rinse under cold water, and place in a medium bowl. Toss with the sesame oil. Set aside.

Fill a shallow bowl with at least 1 inch of room temperature water. Put a clean kitchen towel on a large cutting board next to the bowl. Submerge one piece of rice paper in the water until softened and pliable but not falling apart, about 20 seconds. Place on the kitchen towel.

Arrange a few pieces of each vegetable along the lower third (the edge closest to you), leaving 1 inch around the perimeter of the rice paper unfilled.

Sprinkle the vegetables with the herbs and edible flowers.

Roll up the rice paper like a burrito: Fold the lower edge up tightly over the filling, then fold the sides inward and over the filling. Then finish rolling. Place seam side down. Cover with a damp kitchen towel while you repeat with the remaining ingredients. Transfer the rolls to a serving platter, sprinkle with flowers, and serve the dipping sauces alongside.

Peanut Sauce

½ cup smooth peanut butter

3 tablespoons low-sodium soy sauce or tamari

2 tablespoons rice vinegar

2 tablespoons honey

1 tablespoon toasted sesame oil

1 to 2 cloves garlic, minced

In a small bowl, whisk together the peanut butter, soy sauce, vinegar, honey, sesame oil, and garlic. Whisk in enough water (about 3 tablespoons) to make a smooth sauce.

Nuoc Cham

½ cup fresh lime juice (from 4 limes)

½ cup sugar

⅓ cup fish sauce

1 to 2 cloves garlic, minced

1 red chile, minced, or 1 teaspoon sambal oelek

In a small bowl, whisk together the lime juice, sugar, fish sauce, garlic, red chili, and 1 cup water until the sugar dissolves.

Soy-Ginger Sesame Sauce

2 scallions, thinly sliced

1 clove garlic, minced

¼ cup soy sauce

2 teaspoons honey

½ teaspoon grated ginger

½ teaspoon toasted sesame oil

In a small bowl, whisk together the scallions, garlic, soy sauce, honey, ginger, and sesame oil until thoroughly combined.

Street Corn on the Cob

Summer corn is a Vineyard obsession. Restaurant menus are peppered with corn dishes all season long, while eager shoppers at the farmers market practically elbow other early birds out of the way for the perfect cob. At Beach Road overlooking lovely Lagoon Pond, chef Frank Williams chooses Morning Glory Farm's irresistibly sweet corn and pulls from his memory bank of travels. Inspired by Mexico's popular street snack elote, with a layover in Korea for their sweet, fruity chilies that bring a delicious tang, this corn is a messy, creamy, textural delight. Eat with your hands!

SERVES 4

1 cup mayonnaise

2 tablespoons gochujang (Korean chili paste)

1 small clove garlic, grated

¾ teaspoon gochugaru (Korean red pepper flakes), plus more for garnish

Finely grated zest and juice of ½ lime

4 ears corn, shucked

1 cup cotija cheese, crumbled

Cilantro leaves for garnish

1 lime, quartered

In a medium bowl, whisk together the mayonnaise, gochujang, garlic, ¾ teaspoon gochugaru, and lime zest and juice. Refrigerate until ready to use and up to 3 days.

Preheat a grill to high. Grill the corn until char marks appear here and there on every side, 1 to 2 minutes per side. Be careful not to overcook—you want the corn to stay juicy and crunchy. Transfer the grilled corn to a baking sheet. Once the corn is cool enough to handle (any warmer and the mayonnaise will slide off), arrange it on a large platter and slather each cob with the mayonnaise mixture. Top with gochugaru, cotija, and cilantro. Serve with lime wedges.

Stuffed Squash

THE LARDER, VINEYARD HAVEN

This is a dish destined for cozy fall suppers by a crackling fireplace, and it is easily customizable depending on guests or mood. Sub the herbs with whichever are still lingering from your summer garden, or leave out the sausage and bulk up the grains for a meat-free centerpiece that can easily take pride of place at your Thanksgiving table. You can also use barley, quinoa, wild rice, brown rice, or a combination of grains in place of the farro. Adjust the amount of stock or water to cook the grain of your choice.

SERVES 4 TO 6

1 butternut or other winter squash, halved and seeded

1 tablespoon plus 1½ teaspoons extra virgin olive oil

Kosher salt and freshly ground black pepper

1 cup chopped kale, chard, or collards

½ medium yellow onion, diced

½ large red bell pepper, chopped

3 cloves garlic, minced

2 to 3 tablespoons mixed fresh herbs, such as thyme, rosemary, and oregano

1 cup farro

3 cups vegetable stock or water

½ cup dry white wine

½ pound pork sausage, casings removed (omit for a meat-free version)

Crushed red pepper flakes (optional)

Grated Parmigiano Reggiano for sprinkling

Preheat the oven to 375°F. Line a medium baking sheet with parchment paper. Brush the cut sides of the squash with 1½ teaspoons olive oil and season with salt and pepper. Roast, cut sides down, until tender, 45 minutes to 1 hour.

Meanwhile, heat the remaining 1 tablespoon olive oil in a large, heavy-bottomed skillet over medium heat. Sauté the kale, onion, bell pepper, garlic, and herbs until softened, about 8 minutes. Add the farro and toast for 1 minute to absorb the flavors. Add the stock and wine, bring to a boil, reduce the heat to low, and cover. Cook until the liquid has been absorbed and the farro is tender but still has some chew, about 25 minutes.

While the farro simmers, brown the sausage in a small skillet over medium heat, breaking it up with a spoon, until cooked through, 5 minutes. Drain the excess fat.

Remove the squash from the oven and reduce the heat to 350°F. When the squash is cool enough to handle, scoop out some of the flesh, leaving a ¾-inch border along the sides and bottom. Chop the flesh and reserve.

When the farro is cooked, stir in the sausage and reserved squash flesh. Season with salt and pepper and with red pepper flakes, if using. Fill the squash shells with the stuffing, top with Parmigiano, and bake until the cheese has melted, about 10 minutes. Serve hot.

Walkaway Beets
with Citrus Dressing

SUSIE MIDDLETON, WEST TISBURY

Susie Middleton really, *really* loves vegetables. The farmer/author/editor always seems to be finding new ways with local produce, inspiring her *Cook the Vineyard* readers with adventures of farmstand hopping on the hunt for seasonal treasures (read more opposite). Susie's enthusiasm makes you feel like you're right there with her as she gets the inside scoop on a unique variety of radicchio or when the first new potatoes will hit the markets. Without playing favorites, sweet and earthy beets are on frequent rotation at home in West Tisbury, so she developed this versatile recipe for perfect roasted beets every time. Roasting them en papillote, or in a foil pouch with aromatics, gifts you with a parcel of autumnal deliciousness, and it's largely hands-off. Enjoy beets warm in this salad alongside a Sunday roast, or refrigerate with the dressing for a mid-week lunch. For this option, bulk up with greens or grains and something creamy—feta, goat cheese, a dollop of labneh. Or stack onto crostini with a trickle of aged balsamic. As a bonus, Susie says there's no need to peel the beets as the skin is perfectly edible. Less waste, less fuss—win-win.

SERVES 4

1 pound beets, washed but not peeled and ends trimmed

4 large shallots, peeled and quartered lengthwise with stem ends intact

3 tablespoons extra virgin olive oil

6 sprigs thyme

¾ teaspoon kosher salt, plus more to taste

2 teaspoons finely grated lemon or orange zest

1 tablespoon fresh lemon juice

1 tablespoon fresh orange juice

½ teaspoon rice wine vinegar

½ teaspoon maple syrup or honey

2 teaspoons roughly chopped cilantro, basil, flat-leaf parsley leaves, and/or dill

2 tablespoons chopped toasted walnuts (pistachios or hazelnuts work great, too)

Preheat the oven to 375°F. Place a large piece of foil on a large baking sheet.

Cut the beets into equal-size pieces: baby beets can be quartered or cut into wedges; larger beets can be sliced in half horizontally and then cut into wedges. Toss the beets, shallots, olive oil, thyme, and ¾ teaspoon salt together in a medium bowl. Transfer to the center of the foil and fold up the foil. Crimp the edges to seal.

Roast for 1½ hours, then carefully check for doneness. Lift the foil away from one edge, avoiding the steam, and skewer one or two beets with the tip of a paring knife. If the knife slides in easily, they're done. If not (and they often need more time), reseal the foil package and continue cooking until tender, checking at 15-minute intervals.

Meanwhile, in a small bowl whisk together the citrus zest and juices, vinegar, maple syrup, and salt to taste.

In a bowl, toss the beets and shallots with the dressing. Just before serving, sprinkle with chopped herbs and nuts.

Susie Middleton

Susie Middleton is the editor of *Cook the Vineyard*, the *Vineyard Gazette*'s always-inspiring cooking website and newsletter. Previously, she worked in restaurants, was chief editor of *Fine Cooking* magazine, and started Green Island Farm in West Tisbury. She is the author of four cookbooks. Today, her passion is growing flowers on the farm she shares with her husband.

I feel so blessed to live here. I'm up early every day to walk Farmer, our sweet dog, and to harvest my flowers. On a perfect day, I have breakfast at ArtCliff Diner. Gina Stanley is wonderful, and there's always a delicious special or two. Then I'll head up-island for some farmstand hopping. I'll pop into The Grey Barn, Beetlebung, and North Tabor Farm to say hi to the pigs, and pick up their beautiful produce. But generally, I come to chat with the farmers, hear what they're excited about, and seek inspiration for my upcoming columns.

I collect my goodies and spend the afternoon back in my kitchen testing recipes. I focus on technique, so exploring a new method for seasonal produce and sharing it with our readers brings me a lot of joy. I test a lot of recipes and I'm lucky because my husband is an enthusiastic taster!

We'll go out for dinner, to State Road if we want to stay local, or to the bar at l'étoile. It's so cozy there. Coffee and chocolate are two things I can't live without, so after dinner we'll stop at the Ice Cream and Candy Bazaar for a scoop of mocha chip.

We finish as we do every day, with a long walk. It could be a stroll through Flat Point, or the woods, or the beach. We have to spend time in nature every day. If the day ends outside under the stars, well, to me that's a truly perfect day.

Soups & Salads

Portuguese Holy Ghost Soup
(Sopa do Espírito Santo)

GINNY COUTINHO, VINEYARD HAVEN

This sopa has been kindly shared by Ginny Coutinho of Vineyard Haven, from her family's sweet recipe booklet. It's a two-part meal, first the broth, bread, and mint, followed by the meat and vegetables. While every family has its own recipe, sopa is an integral part of the Holy Ghost Feast, hosted by the Portuguese-American Club every July since the 1930s. The Feast honors thirteenth-century Queen Isabel, and her kindness to the poor. Following a procession through Oak Bluffs, visitors line up for soup to enjoy at communal tables, the air fragrant with malasadas (doughnuts) fried in oil.

The PA Club began as a private, members-only men's club. "Women were not allowed in until the late 1960s; now it's run by women!" laughs Tricia Bergeron, who served as president for twenty-two years and whose grandfather William cofounded the club. Today, it remains a benevolent society caring for the community that hosts gatherings and fundraisers. The Feast is many things—a reunion for family and friends, the commemoration of religious traditions, and a celebration of shared heritage. Long may it continue.

SERVES 4 TO 6

1 pound bone-in beef shank

1 large yellow onion, chopped

2 teaspoons kosher salt, plus more as needed

Freshly ground black pepper

1 chouriço or linguiça sausage

3 to 4 medium potatoes, peeled

1 medium head green cabbage, cored and cut into bite-size pieces

1 loaf dry, stale Portuguese bread (see Note)

⅓ cup fresh mint leaves

Put the beef shank and onion in a large pot and add cold water to cover by 2 inches. Bring to a boil over medium heat, skimming off any foam, then reduce the heat to low, partially cover the pot, and simmer gently until the meat is tender, about 30 minutes. Add 2 teaspoons salt and taste the broth for seasoning. Add more salt, if necessary, and season with pepper.

Add the chouriço, cover the pot, and cook for 15 additional minutes. Add the potatoes and cabbage and simmer until the potatoes are tender and easily pierced with a knife, about 20 minutes.

With a slotted spoon or skimmer, remove the beef, chouriço, potatoes, and cabbage from the pot and place on a large platter. Slice the bread into small chunks. Make a layer of one-third of the bread on the bottom of a large serving bowl or soup tureen, then top with one-third of the mint leaves. Continue making 2 more layers, ending with a layer of mint on top. Gently ladle the hot broth into the serving bowl and let it sit for 10 minutes to soak the bread.

Ladle the broth, the soaked bread, and mint leaves into individual serving bowls; serve the beef, chouriço, potatoes, and cabbage on a separate platter to enjoy with the soup.

Note: The bread must be dry and stale, so buy or bake a loaf a few days before you intend to serve the soup.

Striped Bass & Clam Chowder

THE HOMEPORT, CHILMARK

Every summer resort destination has that go-to place: the one for birthdays and anniversaries; the one to dazzle visitors with the sunset. The Homeport has been that place on Martha's Vineyard since 1930. Generations have sipped chowder, slurped clams, and rolled up their sleeves with gusto to celebrate the simple joys of summer overlooking Menemsha.

"There are so many special memories here," says Seth Woods, who reopened the restaurant in 2022 with co-owner Eric Burke. "Kids' first oysters, boats pulling in for shore dinners, folks lining up for blueberry cobbler at the back door. It was a rite of passage to work here. That legacy is important to us."

While there's no shortage of chowder up and down New England, there are a few details that make this one a standout. It's creamy but light, a reprieve from chowders that are thick enough to stand a spoon in. They use bacon from The Grey Barn and striped bass and clams from Mike Holtham at The Net Result. In true circular island fashion, Mike's father, Will, owned The Homeport from 1977 to 2009. In Will's charming 2011 cookbook, he recounted that friends once requested a batch of chowder in lieu of a wedding gift. That's the power of a good chowder.

SERVES 4

2 tablespoons unsalted butter, plus more for serving

3 strips bacon, finely diced

1 medium yellow onion, finely diced

1 clove garlic, minced

1 tablespoon all-purpose flour

2 cups chicken stock

2 cups clam juice

1 rib celery, finely diced

1 large golden creamer potato, unpeeled, coarsely diced

1 bay leaf

1 cup heavy cream

1 cup half-and-half

Kosher salt

2 pounds striped bass fillet, skinned and coarsely diced

1 cup shucked raw quahogs, chopped

Leaves of 4 sprigs thyme for garnish

Freshly ground black pepper

Oyster crackers for serving

Melt the 2 tablespoons butter in a medium, heavy-bottomed saucepan over low heat. Add the bacon, onion, and garlic. Cook, covered, for 5 minutes.

Whisk the flour with ½ cup water in a small bowl until no lumps remain. Add the stock, clam juice, celery, potato, bay leaf, and flour mixture to the saucepan and simmer for 15 minutes. Pour in the heavy cream and half-and-half, and bring to a simmer. Taste and adjust salt (if the bacon is very salty you may not need any). Add the bass and quahogs to the pan, remove from the heat, and set aside to rest, covered, for 15 minutes. (The bass and clams will cook in the residual heat.)

Divide the chowder among individual serving bowls. Garnish with thyme, season with pepper, and top each portion with a knob of butter. Serve oyster crackers on the side.

Tip: If you can't find quahogs use cherrystones or littleneck clams.

Tomato & Watermelon Gazpacho

The vibe at Alchemy is fancy without the fuss. There is real finesse with the menu and cocktails, and each floor offers a different experience: the jovial first-floor bar and bistro, an elegant dining room made for celebrations, and a cozy upstairs complete with fireplace. Maybe that's why it's been an Edgartown mainstay for over twenty years. Or it could be because of executive chef and owner Christoper Stam's love of locally sourced ingredients. This is the no-cook soup of the summer, made with the season's sweetest tomatoes and watermelon, cool and refreshing after a day on the beach. Ready in minutes, it's also an ideal dinner party welcome course. Arrange the garnishes in individual bowls, so guests can help themselves.

SERVES 6 TO 8

5 medium tomatoes, coarsely chopped

5 (3-inch-square) pieces watermelon, rind and seeds removed

3 cloves garlic

1 shallot

2 tablespoons honey or agave syrup

3 teaspoons A.1. Steak Sauce

1 to 2 teaspoons Tabasco

¼ cup red wine vinegar

¼ cup vegetable oil

Kosher salt and freshly ground black pepper

Crumbled feta, sliced jalapeño, chopped mint, and crushed red pepper flakes for garnish

Extra virgin olive oil for finishing

In a high-speed blender, blend the tomatoes, watermelon, garlic, shallot, honey, A.1. Steak Sauce, Tabasco, and vinegar until smooth.

While blending on high speed, add the vegetable oil in a thin stream. Blend until emulsified. The soup should be smooth and have a creamy texture. Season with salt and pepper. Refrigerate and serve chilled. Serve garnishes and olive oil on the side.

Vineyard Cioppino

It's fitting that cioppino, that luscious Italian-American fish soup so iconic to San Francisco, has a counterpart on seafood-loving Martha's Vineyard. Richard Doucette, executive chef of The Dunes, creates a rich tomato broth heady with fennel and saffron, then spikes it with smoky chouriço (a spiced Portuguese sausage popular in New England) and a medley of fresh, regional seafood. Make sure to have garlic bread on hand to mop up the delicious juices.

SERVES 4

½ cup extra virgin olive oil

½ cup minced shallot

6 cloves garlic, sliced

1 bulb fennel, cored, trimmed, and finely diced

Kosher salt

1 (28-ounce) can whole peeled San Marzano tomatoes, crushed by hand

¼ cup tomato paste

Pinch saffron threads

Pinch crushed red pepper flakes

1 cup white wine

2 cups clam juice

1 tablespoon fish sauce

3 sprigs flat-leaf parsley

3 sprigs thyme

Freshly ground black pepper

1 large chouriço sausage, halved, or 2 Spanish chorizo sausages

1½ pounds littleneck clams, cleaned

1½ pounds mussels, cleaned

½ pound calamari, sliced

½ pound large shrimp, peeled and deveined

2 sprigs rosemary

Heat the olive oil in a Dutch oven over medium-low heat. Add the shallot, garlic, and fennel, season well with salt, and cook until translucent, about 5 minutes.

Add the crushed tomatoes, tomato paste, saffron, and red pepper flakes. Cook for 1 minute. Pour in the white wine and deglaze, scraping the bottom of the pot. Add the clam juice, fish sauce, parsley, thyme, and black pepper. Cook, stirring occasionally, until the liquid is reduced by half, 10 to 15 minutes. Taste and adjust seasoning.

Cook the chouriço in a medium, heavy-bottomed skillet or on the grill over medium heat for 5 minutes, turning halfway through. Add the chouriço to the broth, then the clams, mussels, calamari, shrimp, and rosemary. Cover and steam until the mussels and clams have opened (discard any that do not) and the calamari and shrimp are cooked through, 6 to 8 minutes. Slice the chouriço into quarters and return to the pot. Remove and discard rosemary, parsley, and thyme. Divide among 4 individual serving bowls and serve hot.

Corn & Heirloom Tomato Salad
with Honey-Herb Vinaigrette

MORNING GLORY FARM, EDGARTOWN

Sorry, Christmas, Morning Glory Farm's sweet corn harvest is the most wonderful time of the year. The harvest generally starts in mid- to late July and continues bestowing us with corn, glorious corn, through mid-October. Each ear is hand-selected at peak ripeness and you can still feel the warmth of the sun on just-picked corn at the MoGlo farmstand. That is, if there are any ears left (it can be a bit of a blood sport to secure the prized crop). The sentiment echoed among shoppers is that there's nothing else like it, even on the mainland. There is island pride in its provenance.

This simple, colorful salad, from Morning Glory Farm's executive chef, Augustus Paquet-Whall, highlights two of the stars of summer: corn and tomatoes (the third is strawberries, see page 45). His philosophy in the kitchen is to be intentional with ingredients—and with corn this good, there's no need to overcomplicate things. Raw sweet corn is not only safe to eat but packed with nutrients and pure corn flavor. Serve alongside grilled meat or seafood, or enjoy a big bowl all on its own.

SERVES 4

Vinaigrette

1 small shallot, finely chopped

¼ cup sherry vinegar

3 tablespoons honey, such as Island Bee Company or Black Brook

1 teaspoon Dijon mustard, such as Uncle Neil's

¾ cup plus 2 tablespoons light olive oil

½ cup roughly chopped leafy green herbs, such as basil, flat-leaf parsley, tarragon, dill, and/or mint

Kosher salt and freshly ground black pepper

Salad

6 ears corn, shucked

2 large, ripe heirloom tomatoes, chopped

4 ounces feta, such as Mermaid Farm

Make the vinaigrette: In a medium bowl, combine the shallot with the sherry vinegar. Let sit for 10 minutes to soften the sharpness of the shallot. Whisk in the honey and mustard until incorporated. Add the oil in a thin stream, whisking constantly, until emulsified. Stir in the herbs and season with salt and pepper.

Make the salad: Cut the corn off the cob into a large bowl (see method in Fresh Corn Polenta with Tomato Jam recipe, page 120). Use the back of a knife to scrape the corn milk from the cob. Add the tomatoes, then crumble the feta on top.

Toss the salad with vinaigrette. Taste and adjust seasoning. Enjoy at room temperature or chilled.

The Empress & the Conch Salad

Chef Deon Thomas is the king of conch, and he's on a mission to put conch (pronounced *conk*) on the map—and on the menu. With a briny-sweet flavor and chewy texture, reminiscent of scallops and calamari, conch is popular in the Caribbean and is native to the Vineyard waters, where the local species is known as the channeled whelk. The Wampanoag collected conch, as did Azorean fishers. Today, however, local conch is exported to Asia, and Deon is committed to working with fishermen around Cape Cod to source the delicious meat. (Frozen conch meat can be purchased online if you can't access fresh conch where you are.) His menu at Chef Deon's Kitchen, and at the many events he caters, features conch in a variety of ways—chowder, fritters, even meatballs. This salad is bright and refreshing, made for enjoying with your toes in the sand. "This dish is the heartbeat of the islands," shares Deon, "enjoyed any time of the day, served over salad greens, or with extra scotch bonnet and an ice-cold Red Stripe." Deon served this appetizer at a James Beard Foundation dinner on Martha's Vineyard. In it, the conch is dressed with indigo-hued Empress 1908 gin—hence the name.

Deon's story is as colorful as his cooking. Growing up in Jamaica, he learned to cook alongside the women of his family. He launched his career in the Hamptons and quickly became a three-island chef, moving from Long Island to Anguilla, where he was lured to Martha's Vineyard. "Home is where the heart is," says Deon, "and I love this island home." Classically trained at the Culinary Institute of America, Deon opened a number of beloved restaurants across the island, and today you'll find him at the VFW, flexing between Caribbean and American cuisines. And conch is always on the menu. Despite being one of the busiest chefs on the island, he always makes time to give back. Every year, he and his volunteers prepare free Thanksgiving meals for the community with all the trimmings. "That's the Vineyard way," he smiles.

Deon's tips for preparing fresh conch:

- Don't steam or boil conch in the shell, as this will cook the meat with its guts and muddy the flavor.

- Freeze conch for one day in the shell, and the meat will come out in one piece.

- Peel the skin and remove the guts. Separate the tenders for salad (or sear over high heat like scallops), and save the harder muscle for chowder or fritters.

SERVES 4

1 pound conch tenders	¼ cup chopped cilantro leaves
Finely grated zest and juice of 1 lemon	¾ cup diced fresh pineapple
2 tablespoons extra virgin olive oil	½ cup diced bell pepper
Kosher salt and freshly ground black pepper	½ cup diced sweet onion
2 tablespoons Empress 1908 indigo gin	Lemon wedges for serving
½ scotch bonnet pepper, minced	

Cut the conch tenders into a small dice. Place in a bowl, cover, and refrigerate while you prepare the rest of the dish.

Whisk the lemon zest and juice and the olive oil in a small bowl until emulsified, then season with salt and pepper and 1 tablespoon of the gin. Add the scotch bonnet.

In a separate medium bowl, combine the cilantro, pineapple, bell pepper, and onion. Drizzle the lemon juice mixture over the pineapple mixture and toss to combine. Taste and adjust seasoning.

Add the diced conch to the bowl and gently toss to combine. Avoid overmixing so the conch stays vibrant. Allow to rest at room temperature for 5 minutes, then transfer to a serving bowl. Sprinkle on the remaining 1 tablespoons gin. Serve with lemon wedges.

Kale Salad
with Feta, Almonds & Garlicky Honey-Mustard Dressing

MERMAID FARM, CHILMARK

"The feta is reason alone to come to MV," declares an online reviewer of Mermaid Farm, and they're not wrong. Mermaid Farm feta is otherworldly—the creamiest you're likely to taste, briny like the ocean minutes away. The finest eateries proudly boast about having Mermaid Farm feta on their menus. Technically, it's feta-style cheese, as it's made using milk from the farm's Jersey cows instead of the traditional sheep's and goat's milk.

Generational islanders Caitlin Jones and Allan Healy started their Middle Road vegetable farm in 1997. They soon expanded it into a raw-milk dairy so they could offer their boys high-quality milk, yogurt, and cheese. Their farmstand is the kind of honor-system hidden gem off the side of a country road that you daydream about. Look for the sign that says FETA and pull in immediately, although if you happen to miss out (the feta obsession is real), other dairy delights await—cream-on-top yogurt, velvety lassis, and fluffy fromage. Because farm work never stops, these busy farmers tend to graze whenever they have a moment, but this crunchy kale salad is a favorite worth sitting down for. Pair with Allen Farm's lamb and feta meatballs (page 187) to enjoy the feta's unique tang two ways; add roasted squash and farro to make the salad even more substantial.

SERVES 4 TO 6

Salad

2 bunches curly kale

2 tablespoons extra virgin olive oil

6 ounces feta, such as Mermaid Farm, broken into big chunks

¼ medium red onion, thinly sliced

⅓ cup roasted almonds, roughly chopped

Dressing

3 tablespoons extra virgin olive oil

Juice of 1 small lemon

1 small shallot, minced

2 teaspoons raw honey, such as Black Brook or Island Bee Company

2 teaspoons Dijon mustard

1 large clove garlic, minced

¼ teaspoon kosher salt

Pinch freshly ground black pepper

Make the salad: Remove the stems of the kale leaves and tear the leaves into bite-size pieces. Place in a large bowl. Drizzle with 2 tablespoons olive oil and massage with your hands for about 30 seconds to break down the fibrous leaves. Add most of the feta along with the red onion and almonds and toss gently, being careful not to break up the feta chunks too much.

Make the dressing: Combine all the ingredients in a glass jar with a lid. Shake for 10 seconds to emulsify.

Pour three-quarters of the dressing over the salad and toss to combine. Taste, and if you like more dressing, add the rest; otherwise, leftovers can be stored in the refrigerator for up to 2 days. Top with the remaining feta and serve.

Lobster Cobb Salad

WATERSIDE MARKET, VINEYARD HAVEN

There are salads and then there are salads! This is the latter, with an abundance of fresh lobster happily crashing the classic Cobb party. If you're looking to get your lobster fix, look no further than Waterside Market, the year-round café that is a popular pit stop for those fresh off the ferry. In addition to the lobster Cobb, Waterside Market offers lobster rolls, club sandwiches, and Benedicts, for a decadent start to the day. There's a generous amount of lobster in the salad, so adjust it according to your level of extravagance.

SERVES 4

½ cup mayonnaise

½ cup full-fat sour cream

½ cup buttermilk

1 tablespoon fresh lemon juice

1 teaspoon dried dill

½ teaspoon dried parsley

½ teaspoon dried chives

¼ teaspoon onion powder

¼ teaspoon garlic powder

¼ teaspoon finely ground black pepper

4 cups mixed greens

1½ pounds cooked lobster meat, coarsely chopped

8 ounces bacon, finely diced and cooked until crisp

2 avocados, pitted, peeled, and thinly sliced

2 medium tomatoes, diced

4 hard-boiled eggs, peeled and halved

¾ cup crumbled blue cheese

1 lemon, quartered

1 tablespoon snipped chives

In a medium bowl, whisk the mayonnaise, sour cream, buttermilk, lemon juice, dried herbs, onion powder, garlic powder, and black pepper to combine. Refrigerate until ready to use and up to 1 week.

Assemble the salad by placing 1 cup mixed greens in each of 4 individual bowls. Divide the lobster, bacon, avocado, tomato, eggs, blue cheese, and lemon quarters evenly among the bowls, keeping each element separate. Scatter on the chives and serve the dressing on the side.

Peach Salad

MV SALADS, OAK BLUFFS

The world could do with a little more kindness. That's the philosophy of Susanna Herlitz-Ferguson, owner of MV Salads, a feel-good salad bar on Circuit Avenue (there's another in Edgartown). The daily menu reflects collaboration with local farms and features Susanna's own salad dressing—a family recipe of vinegar, herbs, and spices that she began bottling after her loyal customers begged her to. This salad is great with feta or grilled halloumi, and if you'd like to add protein, marinate chicken or tofu in MV The Dressing before cooking.

SERVES 4 TO 6

1 (8-ounce) bottle MV The Dressing (or 8 ounces white balsamic vinaigrette)

½ avocado, pitted and peeled

¼ cup mayonnaise

1 tablespoon lime juice

8 cups arugula and mixed spring greens

4 watermelon radishes or 8 red radishes, thinly sliced

4 peaches, pitted and thinly sliced

4 tablespoons flaked almonds

Mint leaves for garnish

In a blender, purée the dressing, avocado, mayonnaise, and lime juice.

Place the greens in a bowl. Add some of the dressing and toss to combine. Arrange the radish slices on top, the peach slices on top of the radish, and sprinkle with almonds. Drizzle with more dressing to taste and garnish with mint leaves.

Radicchio Panzanella

BEETLEBUNG FARM, CHILMARK

Beetlebung Farm, farmed for 250 years by generations of the Fischer family, has a special place in the hearts of islanders. Today the small-scale farm is stewarded by The Farm Group and comanagers Kate Woods and Nick Doherty. They employ regenerative agriculture practices to grow a diverse inventory of vegetables, herbs, and flowers, some of them new to even the most curious cook (seek out their tango celery and sweet hakurei turnips, if you can; they're incredible).

Sharing knowledge of the land is part of Beetlebung's ethos, and during summer evenings, guests can mingle with Kate and Nick to dive deep into their many varieties of tomatoes, peas, cucumbers, and more while rubbing elbows at communal dinners that celebrate humble ingredients. And while summer produce is lauded, it's fall and winter vegetables, like radicchio, that really excite these young farmers. "I think we're often taught that bitter equals bad," says Kate. "But if you know how to work *with* the bitter and balance it, you can unlock a whole other part of your palate that you might not have known otherwise."

Think of this very "rad" salad as the first date in your love affair with bitter, offset by crispy onions and a creamy, punchy dressing.

SERVE 6 TO 8

4 small yellow onions

1½ cups olive oil

1 loaf focaccia or sourdough bread

½ cup fromage frais, chèvre, or feta

2 tablespoons chopped thyme or marjoram, plus more for garnish

3 cloves garlic, minced

1 anchovy

1 tablespoon capers

3 tablespoons red wine vinegar

Kosher salt and freshly ground black pepper

4 heads Chioggia radicchio, halved through the root ends and sliced crosswise into strips

Preheat the oven to 425°F.

Slice the onions. (A mandoline is very useful for this—set to medium thickness, not paper-thin.) Pour the olive oil into a medium saucepan and add the onion slices. Cook over medium-low heat, stirring often, until lightly browned, 25 to 30 minutes. Remove the onions with a slotted spoon and place on a plate lined with paper towels to drain; they will crisp up as they cool. Reserve the oil and set aside to cool.

Rip the loaf of bread into bite-size pieces and toss with ¼ cup plus 1 tablespoon of the cooled oil. Scatter on a baking sheet and toast in the preheated oven until browned in parts and crisp on the outside but still soft in the center, about 10 minutes.

In a food processor or blender combine the fromage frais, 2 tablespoons of the reserved oil, 2 tablespoons thyme, garlic, anchovy, capers, and vinegar and blend until emulsified. Season with salt and pepper.

Place the radicchio in a large bowl and toss with the dressing. Add the croutons and toss again. Top with the crispy onions and garnish with thyme. The salad can rest at room temperature while you prepare the rest of your meal; it only gets better as the bread soaks up the dressing.

Smoked Bluefish Caesar Salad

MARTHA'S VINEYARD SMOKEHOUSE, WEST TISBURY

Bluefish is a favorite on Martha's Vineyard, especially when smoked and featured in a showstopping salad like this one. Friends Nate Gould and Gus Leaf launched their smokehouse in 2014, and the quality of their product is unmatched. Vineyard local Gus catches almost all the fish they use, bleeding and icing the fish immediately, which results in fresher-tasting fillets. With a rich and intensely flavored fish like bluefish, protecting the character of the meat makes all the difference. Chef Nate has perfected the long, slow hickory smoke that allows the fish to shine. Boat to smoke, as they say. Their smoked fish, chowders, and spreads sell out every week at the farmers market, served at porch parties and potlucks. A great salad is all about the textures, and this salad has it in spades. Devour on its own or with grilled sourdough. Don't want to light the grill? Good news: you can broil the romaine instead.

SERVES 2 TO 4

5 anchovy fillets, packed in oil, minced

3 cloves garlic, finely grated

1 egg yolk

Finely grated zest and juice of 1 lemon

1½ teaspoons Dijon mustard

¼ cup avocado oil

¼ cup grated Parmesan, plus more for finishing

Kosher salt and freshly ground black pepper

2 slices day-old sourdough bread, crusts removed and torn

2 tablespoons extra virgin olive oil, plus more for grilling

1 teaspoon caraway seeds, toasted and ground

2 romaine hearts, quartered lengthwise through stems

6 ounces smoked bluefish fillet, such as Martha's Vineyard Smokehouse, picked for any bones

1 tablespoon snipped chives

Flaky sea salt, such as Maldon, for finishing

Combine the anchovies, garlic, egg yolk, lemon juice, and mustard and whisk until smooth. Add the avocado oil in a thin stream while whisking until emulsified. Add ¼ cup Parmesan and season with salt and pepper.

Preheat the oven to 400°F. Heat a grill to its highest heat setting.

Toss the sourdough pieces, 2 tablespoons olive oil, and caraway on a medium baking sheet. Season with salt and pepper. Toast until golden, 8 to 12 minutes, and allow to cool. In a food processor fitted with the metal blade, pulse into coarse crumbs.

Brush the cut sides of the romaine hearts with olive oil and grill to char the outside without overcooking the lettuce, about 45 seconds. Alternatively, preheat the broiler and broil for 2 minutes per side.

Arrange the romaine on a plate and drizzle with some of the dressing. Flake the bluefish on top, followed by the breadcrumbs. Scatter on the chives, lemon zest, and Parmesan. Season with flaky salt and black pepper. Drizzle on the remaining dressing and serve immediately.

Summer Farm Salad

V. JAIME HAMLIN & SONS CATERING,
VINEYARD HAVEN

This salad has it all: crisp Beetlebung Farm greens, sweet tomatoes from Morning Glory Farm, prized Goldbud nectarines, milky mozzarella, and crunchy toasted pine nuts. All kissed with a sparkling vinaigrette. It's the most requested salad served at the star-studded weddings and parties catered by the queen of Vineyard events, V. Jaime Hamlin, and her sons Nick, Alex, and Duncan. A note on Goldbud nectarines: Don't be tempted to substitute regular nectarines. This perfect stone fruit, intoxicatingly fragrant, arrives in July for a very limited time at an eye-watering price. But the taste, especially in this summer salad, will linger in your memory for years.

SERVES 4 TO 6

1 ripe peach, pitted, peeled, and roughly chopped

1 clove garlic

3 tablespoons Champagne vinegar

1 tablespoon honey

1½ teaspoons Dijon mustard

1 teaspoon kosher salt

¼ teaspoon freshly ground black pepper

1 cup extra virgin olive oil

6 cups arugula and mixed greens

2 medium to large red tomatoes, cut into wedges

2 medium to large yellow tomatoes, cut into wedges

2 Goldbud nectarines, pitted and sliced

6 ounces bocconcini

½ cup toasted pine nuts

Blend the peach, garlic, vinegar, honey, mustard, salt, and pepper in a blender until smooth, then add the olive oil in a thin stream while blending and continue until the vinaigrette is emulsified. Taste and adjust seasoning.

Layer the salad greens on a large platter, followed by the tomatoes, nectarines, and mozzarella. Sprinkle with the pine nuts.

Drizzle vinaigrette lightly over the salad just before serving. Serve additional vinaigrette on the side.

V. Jaime Hamlin

V. Jaime Hamlin has catered thousands of events—
from weddings to fundraisers to presidential
birthdays—with her sons Nick, Alex, and Duncan.
Their food reflects Jaime's personal style:
memorable, elegant, and creative. It all started
when Jaime joined her sister, Cynthia, on the island
in the mid-1970s. She made her mark at Martha's
Restaurant, before opening Feasts and The Oyster
Bar with her now ex-husband, Raymond Schilcher.
From there, she began catering the most lavish
of Vineyard parties with her sons, and she hasn't
looked back. Summer and fall are her busiest
seasons, but she still finds moments to enjoy the
bounty of the island.

My perfect Vineyard day always begins with an iced
coffee under our crabapple tree in Vineyard Haven,
making a list of the ingredients I need to pick up at
the farmers market for dinner with friends. After
a sunny drive to the market, I head straight to Tea
Lane's farmstand for some glorious lilies and whatever
other seasonal flower Krishana Collins may be
growing for the dinner table. I pick up Beetlebung
Farm greens from the lovely Kate Woods, fresh
herbs, Morning Glory Farm tomatoes and Butter and
Sugar corn, and a Grey Barn boule.

Then we head up to Menemsha for fresh
swordfish at Larsen's, which I serve with a tomato-
caper sauce that is beautiful with the meaty fish,
corn pudding, and Summer Farm Salad (opposite).

After dropping off the groceries, we pick up
sandwiches and drinks at 7a Foods, then trek up to
Quansoo for a swim and a relaxing afternoon on the
beach. The sun, the sea, and the sand are a tonic!

Back at home, I like to set the table with colorful
Provençal linens and Krishana's gorgeous bouquets.
As friends arrive in the early evening, bathed in
golden light, we toast—with vodka-basil limeade—to
the bounty of summer, the sweetness of friendship,
and this island that we so love.

Mains

15-Ingredient Pork Ribs

FORK TO PORK, VINEYARD HAVEN

Fork to Pork is a local success story helmed by the impressive Jo Douglas. After spending childhood summers on the island, Jo dreamed of returning to farm, and she turned her concern for food waste and livestock well-being into her passion project. Food waste is a global issue, with around 30 percent of food lost or not consumed. The Fork to Pork concept is circular and sustainable: restaurants give their leftovers a second chance, pigs enjoy quality food while grazing and socializing, unlike their industrially raised counterparts, and there's no need to import grain. "It brings me so much joy to care for my own animals and produce high-quality food for my island community" shares Jo, on the land she leases in Tisbury from the Land Bank (cattle in her Leaf to Beef venture graze on pastures in Edgartown). Jo's philosophy is one to embrace: choose the best meat you can afford, even if you eat less of it.

Mornings are spent driving across the island to rescue scrap from partner restaurants. When Jo arrives back at the farm, the piggy excitement is palpable (imagine your pet welcoming you home, multiplied). On the menu? Anything from fresh corn to kale and doughnuts, snouts promptly covered in sprinkles. Soon after feasting, the squeals subside as the pigs collapse into a blissful food coma, sometimes using a pastry as a pillow. Over the spring and summer, they'll gain a pound a day, fattening up to a weight of two hundred pounds. Jo's loyal customers then claim whole pigs to feature proudly on their menus. "Minimizing waste is something that's always on our minds," says chef Al Said of The Covington. "As an example, we go through a ton of Parmesan. The rinds go in our Fork to Pork scrap bucket to feed island pigs that we can then buy and serve."

These succulent pork ribs are the specialty of Jo's dad. They're made every August for a friend's birthday, with Jo supplying the pork. The rub is enough for one (with leftovers that you can use to make barbecue sauce).

MAKES 1-2 RACKS; SERVES 4-8

1 or 2 racks pork ribs

1 cup brown sugar

3 tablespoons chili powder

2 tablespoons paprika

1 tablespoon kosher salt

1 teaspoon freshly ground black pepper

1 teaspoon garlic powder

1 teaspoon onion powder

1 teaspoon ground allspice

1 teaspoon ground cardamom

1 teaspoon cayenne pepper

1 teaspoon celery salt

1 teaspoon ground cinnamon

1 teaspoon ground cloves

1 teaspoon ground coriander

Remove the thin membrane that runs along the back of the rack of ribs by piercing the membrane with a knife and peeling it off.

Combine the brown sugar and all of the seasonings and spices in a medium bowl. Set the ribs on a baking sheet and apply the rub liberally to both sides of the ribs. Allow the flavors to infuse for at least 1 hour at room temperature, or cover and refrigerate for up to 24 hours. (If the ribs are refrigerated, bring them to room temperature before cooking.)

Preheat a charcoal or gas grill with an indirect heat zone to 300°F. Place the ribs on the grill, meaty side up. Close the lid and cook in indirect heat for 1½ hours, rotating halfway through.

Remove the ribs and wrap in heavy-duty foil. (Careful, as they are hot.) Place back on the indirect heat and cook for 30 additional minutes. Rest the ribs in the foil for 10 minutes before carving. (Alternatively, cook the ribs on a baking sheet in a 300°F oven for 1½ hours, then cover in foil and cook 30 additional minutes. Remove the ribs from the foil and broil until lightly charred in parts, about 5 minutes.)

Use a sharp knife to carve the ribs between the bones and transfer to a platter.

Quick Barbecue Sauce for Ribs: Combine 2 cups ketchup, 1 bottle of beer, 2 tablespoons apple cider vinegar, 2 tablespoons brown sugar, 2 tablespoons honey or maple syrup, and ⅓ cup of the dry rub in a medium saucepan and simmer for 20 minutes.

Bloody Mary Tuna

LOBSTERVILLE, OAK BLUFFS

At Lobsterville, the fresh catch often comes straight off the fishing boats at the harbor below. Perch yourself on the gingerbread deck, adorned with lobster buoys, and soak up the sunset. This tuna is a nod to Oak Bluffs's love for the hangover elixir. Juicy summer tomatoes and the zesty, slap-you-awake flavors of pickled onion, celery, horseradish, and Tabasco make this a dish worth getting out of bed for.

SERVES 4

Horseradish Cream

½ cup full-fat sour cream

1 tablespoon prepared horseradish

1 teaspoon Worcestershire sauce

Salad

1 medium red onion, peeled and very thinly sliced

½ cup distilled white vinegar

1½ tablespoons sugar

1 teaspoon kosher salt

3 heirloom tomatoes, diced

1 rib celery, thinly sliced or shaved on a mandoline

2 tablespoons fresh lemon juice

1 tablespoon snipped chives

Tabasco sauce

Flaky sea salt, such as Maldon

Freshly ground black pepper

Extra virgin olive oil for drizzling

Microgreens for garnish

Tuna

2 tablespoons coarsely ground black pepper

1 pound bluefin or yellowfin tuna

Olive oil for searing

Make the horseradish cream: In a small bowl, combine the sour cream, horseradish, and Worcestershire sauce. Cover and refrigerate until ready to serve. (Can be made up to 1 day in advance.)

Make the salad: Place the sliced onion in a small bowl. In a small microwave-safe bowl, combine the vinegar, sugar, salt, and ½ cup water and microwave until the sugar is dissolved, about 30 seconds. Pour this mixture over the onion. Pickle at room temperature for 30 minutes. (The pickled onion can be made up to 2 weeks in advance; store refrigerated in an airtight container.)

In a medium bowl, toss the tomatoes, celery, pickled onion, lemon juice, and chives to combine. Season with Tabasco, flaky salt, and pepper, then drizzle with olive oil. Set aside.

Make the tuna: Place the pepper on a plate and press the tuna into the pepper, coating each side evenly.

Lightly coat a large, heavy-bottomed skillet with oil and place over medium-high heat for 3 minutes. Sear the tuna all over, 1 to 2 minutes per side. Remove from the pan and allow to rest for 5 minutes, then cut into 1-inch slices.

Fan the tuna onto individual serving plates, with some of the tomato and pickled onion salad on the side. Serve with horseradish cream, and garnish with microgreens.

Chicken Pot Pie

CHILMARK TAVERN, CHILMARK

There are places that both soothe and restore, and Chilmark Tavern is one of them. On stepping through its doors, you're greeted as an old friend. Owner Jenna Petersiel has that generous way about her, and since opening in 2010, she's built a culture around old-fashioned hospitality. Though Chilmark is a dry town, she will happily mix you a drink with your BYOB.

Born during the takeout-only pandemic days of 2020, Chilmark Tavern's chicken pot pie was a gift to the community. "Chef Andrew Burkill and I wanted to offer something comforting, familiar, nostalgic, and, of course, delicious," smiles Jenna. "We had no idea that our customers would not let this idea die."

This is just the dish to get you through the gloomy days of winter. Crack through the buttery, flaky crust with your spoon as if you were eating crème brûlée. Pure comfort awaits within.

MAKES 6 INDIVIDUAL 6- TO 8-INCH POT PIES OR 1 LARGE 12-INCH POT PIE

16 tablespoons (2 sticks) unsalted butter, plus more for pan(s)

2 cups all-purpose flour, plus more for work surface

2 quarts chicken stock

1 tablespoon chopped herbs such as thyme, rosemary, and/or flat-leaf parsley leaves, plus more for garnish

Kosher salt and freshly ground black pepper

2 tablespoons extra virgin olive oil

1 large white onion, finely diced

1 large leek (white and light green parts only), finely diced

2 medium carrots, finely diced

2 ribs celery, finely diced

3 cloves garlic, minced

2 cups shelled English peas or petit pois

1 whole roasted chicken, skin removed and meat picked

14 ounces frozen all-butter puff pastry, thawed according to package instructions

1 large egg

1½ teaspoons whole milk

Melt the butter in a large, heavy-bottomed saucepan over medium heat. Gradually add the 2 cups flour while stirring constantly with a wooden spoon. Continue to cook for 5 minutes, until the mixture resembles a paste. Add the stock in a thin stream in three additions, whisking constantly to incorporate between additions. Bring the mixture to a gentle simmer over low heat and cook, stirring frequently, until no lumps remain and the mixture has thickened and coats the back of a spoon, about 8 minutes. Add the 1 tablespoon herbs and season with salt and pepper. Remove from the heat and set aside while you make the filling.

Preheat the oven to 400°F. Place the olive oil in a large skillet over medium heat and sauté the onion, leek, carrots, celery, and garlic until the onion is translucent and the other vegetables have begun to soften, about 8 minutes. Add the sautéed vegetables to the flour-stock mixture and simmer over low heat for 20 minutes, stirring frequently. Allow to cool slightly, then stir in the peas and the chicken meat.

Unfold the puff pastry on a lightly floured surface and roll out from the center with a rolling pin so it is about 2 inches longer on each side than it was originally. Using a sharp knife, cut a circle or circles 1 inch larger than the top circumference of the pan or pans.

In a small bowl, whisk together the egg and milk.

Lightly butter the sides of the pan(s). If making 1 large pie, spoon the filling into the pan; if making 6, divide the filling among the pans. Place the puff pastry circle(s) over the filling and press against the rim(s) of the pan(s). Brush the top(s) with the egg wash. Use a paring knife to cut a 1-inch vent in the top of each pie. Season with black pepper and sprinkle with herbs. Bake until the puff pastry is golden brown, 15 to 20 minutes for individual pies or 25 to 30 minutes for a large pie.

Cod Cakes
with Lobster Tartar Sauce

LUCKY HANK'S, EDGARTOWN

There are as many recipes for cod cakes as there are for chowder. What makes the cakes at Lucky Hank's one of the most popular dishes? Sweet chunks of poached cod (unlike the stringy shredded cod you'll often find) and the lack of filler, like potato. The signature dish of owner and chef Doug Smith, the cakes, topped with a lobster tartar sauce (that's also fantastic as a filling for deviled eggs), have been on the menu since day one. Once you have these cod cakes in your repertoire, you'll come to depend on them for brunch, lunch, and dinner.

MAKES TEN (4-INCH) CAKES

Lobster Tartar Sauce

1 cup mayonnaise

1 ounce cooked lobster meat, finely diced, about 2 tablespoons

1 tablespoon minced shallot

1 tablespoon capers, drained and chopped

1 tablespoon finely chopped flat-leaf parsley, chives, and tarragon

1 hard-boiled egg, peeled and finely diced

¼ cup sweet relish

¼ cup diced dill pickle

½ teaspoon lemon juice

Kosher salt and freshly ground black pepper

Cod Cakes

2 pounds cod fillet

2 quarts whole milk

2 bay leaves

Kosher salt and freshly ground black pepper

3 scallions, chopped

1 shallot, finely diced

½ small green bell pepper, finely diced and patted dry

½ small red bell pepper, finely diced and patted dry

1 to 2 tablespoons chopped flat-leaf parsley, chives, and tarragon

1 tablespoon dried dill

2 large eggs, lightly beaten

½ cup full-fat sour cream

¼ cup good-quality mayonnaise

2 tablespoons Dijon mustard

2⅓ cups panko breadcrumbs

2 tablespoons unsalted butter

2 tablespoons olive or vegetable oil

Make the lobster tartar sauce: In a small bowl, mix the mayonnaise, lobster meat, shallot, capers, herbs, egg, sweet relish, dill pickles, and lemon juice and season with salt and pepper. Refrigerate in an airtight container for up to 3 days.

Make the cod cakes: Combine the cod, milk, and bay leaves in a medium saucepan. Season with salt and pepper. Place over medium-low heat and cook until the cod whitens and becomes flaky, about 15 minutes. Strain through a fine-mesh sieve, collecting the liquid in a heatproof container. Remove and discard bay leaves. (Once cooled, the poaching liquid can be stored, covered, in the refrigerator for up to 2 days; it makes a great base for chowder.)

In a large bowl, combine the cooked cod, scallions, shallot, bell peppers, herbs, dill, eggs, sour cream, mayonnaise, mustard, and ⅓ cup of the panko. Gently fold to combine without breaking up the cod.

Place the remaining 2 cups panko in a shallow dish. Divide the cod mixture into 10 equal portions and form each into a cake. Place 1 cake in the panko and gently press to coat on all sides. Transfer to a large plate and repeat with remaining cakes. Cover and refrigerate for 1 hour.

In a nonstick skillet large enough to hold 5 cakes in a single layer, combine 1 tablespoon butter and 1 tablespoon oil. Place over medium heat. When the butter has melted, add half of the cakes to the skillet and cook, turning once, until golden brown, about 2 minutes per side. (The cod is already cooked so the cakes just need to get nicely browned.) Transfer to a plate. Add the remaining 1 tablespoon butter and 1 tablespoon oil to the skillet and cook the remaining cakes.

Serve hot with the lobster tartar sauce on the side.

Corn Risotto
with Scallops

The Red Cat has lived many lives. It was first a restaurant in West Tisbury (where you'll now find State Road), before migrating over to Oak Bluffs and the quirky house on Kennebec. Today, the Red Cat has found its home on Circuit Avenue. The constant is chef and owner Ben DeForest, whose finesse with seasonal ingredients has made the restaurant a must-visit on every Vineyard itinerary. Ben is a music lover and the atmosphere is pure rock 'n' roll, with vintage music posters and art. One of the most popular dishes on the menu is a celebration of sweet corn and even sweeter scallops, whether plump sea scallops or the tiny bay scallops of late fall.

SERVES 4

2 tablespoons extra virgin olive oil

4 tablespoons unsalted butter

1 medium yellow onion, halved and thinly sliced into half-moons

1 sprig rosemary

2 cups arborio rice

2 teaspoons kosher salt, plus more to taste

Kernels of 1 ear corn (see corn-shaving instructions, page 120)

½ cup grated Parmigiano Reggiano

Freshly ground black pepper

8 ounces bay scallops or sea scallops, patted dry

Fresh basil leaves, thinly sliced, for garnish

Boil 8 cups of water in a medium saucepan and keep at a simmer. Heat the oil and 2 tablespoons of the butter in a large, heavy-bottomed pot over medium heat. Add the onion and cook, stirring frequently, until softened, about 6 minutes. Add the rosemary and rice and toast the rice, stirring, for 2 minutes. Reduce the heat to medium-low, add 2 cups of the hot water and the 2 teaspoons salt, and cook, stirring frequently, until the rice has absorbed the water, about 5 minutes. Add more hot water, 1 cup at a time, stirring to incorporate between additions, until the rice is cooked just past al dente without a hard, chalky center. Begin to check frequently after 14 minutes. Add the corn, Parmigiano, and 1 tablespoon of the butter. Season with salt and pepper.

Melt the remaining 1 tablespoon butter in a large skillet over medium-high heat. Add the bay scallops and cook without disturbing for 30 seconds, then flip the scallops with tongs and cook another 30 seconds. For sea scallops, cook for 2 minutes without disturbing, then flip and cook another minute.

Divide the risotto among 4 individual serving plates and top each portion with scallops. Garnish with the basil.

Tip: For even more corn flavor, cook the risotto in corn stock instead of water. For the amount needed in this recipe, place 4 corn cobs in a stockpot with 8 cups of water, bring to a boil over medium heat, then reduce to low, and cover and simmer for 2 hours. Remove the cobs and season the stock with salt.

Crépinettes of Allen Farm Lamb
with Port-Onion Jam

L'ÉTOILE, EDGARTOWN

Flowers and fairy lights cast a romantic glow over the patio at l'étoile. Chef and owner Michael Brisson's restaurant is the epitome of fine French dining. Despite the sophisticated menu and decor, there's always an air of conviviality inside. For Michael, hospitality is just as important as the food and wine.

Crépinettes are succulent meat parcels wrapped in caul fat. The preparation ensures that the meat inside stays juicy (much like a sausage casing). A good butcher shop should be able to obtain caul for you, but if you can't procure it, form the meat mixture into patties or mini meatloaves—they will still taste delicious. Port-onion jam lends a delicious sweet-savory element to the dish. If there are leftovers, try it on burgers or alongside a cheese plate.

MAKES 8 CRÉPINETTES; SERVES 8

Jam

2 tablespoons extra virgin olive oil

4 large yellow onions, sliced lengthwise (root to stem)

¼ cup maple syrup

½ cup sherry vinegar

1 bay leaf

1 cup Cabernet Malbec or another hearty red wine

¼ cup ruby port wine

Kosher salt and white pepper

Crépinettes

1¾ pounds ground lamb, such as Allen Farm

¾ pound pork fat, cut into ½-inch cubes

½ cup diced yellow onion

¼ cup diced celery

¼ cup diced carrot

1 clove garlic, minced

⅓ cup flat-leaf parsley leaves, chopped

1 tablespoon chopped fresh rosemary

1 tablespoon green peppercorns in brine, drained

1 tablespoon kosher salt

½ teaspoon coarsely ground black pepper

½ teaspoon crushed red pepper flakes

1 tablespoon extra virgin olive oil

1 pound caul fat, rinsed under cold water

Thyme and rosemary sprigs for garnish

Make the jam: Heat the olive oil and onions in a large, heavy-bottomed skillet over medium heat. Cook, covered and stirring frequently, until translucent, about 10 minutes. Add the maple syrup and continue cooking until lightly golden, pushing the onions to the side of the skillet so the moisture evaporates. Add the sherry vinegar and bay leaf and cook until the liquid is reduced by half, about 2 minutes. Add the red wine and cook until some of the liquid has evaporated but the skillet is not dry, about 7 minutes. Add the port wine and cook for 2 additional minutes. Remove and discard bay leaf. Season with salt and white pepper. Cover to keep warm, or refrigerate and warm again before serving. (Jam will keep in the refrigerator in an airtight container for up to 5 days.)

Make the crépinettes: In a large bowl, mix the ground lamb, pork fat, onion, celery, carrot, garlic, parsley, rosemary, green peppercorns, salt, pepper, and red pepper flakes. Cover and refrigerate for 3 to 4 hours. Pulse the mix in a food processor fitted with a metal blade in batches, or use a meat grinder with the medium hole attachment and grind the meat mixture through it twice.

Preheat the oven to 400°F. Heat the olive oil in a large, heavy-bottomed skillet over medium-high heat. Form a small patty of the mixture and brown it on both sides, about 3 minutes altogether. Taste and adjust seasoning. Remove the skillet from the heat, but do not rinse it out.

Spread the caul fat on a large work surface. Divide the meat mixture into 8 equal portions, about 4½ ounces each. Shape one portion into a flat patty and place it on the caul. Cut a circle of caul around the patty that is 1 to 2 inches larger than it. Fold the caul over the patty to encase it, then flip over and press flat. Place on a large plate and refrigerate as you repeat with the remaining filling and caul.

Return the skillet to medium heat. Add enough crépinettes to fit comfortably, seam sides down, and cook until golden brown, about 2 minutes. Turn the crépinettes and cook for 2 additional minutes. Transfer to a baking sheet. Repeat until all the crépinettes are cooked, then place them in the oven until cooked through, 5 to 7 minutes. Allow them to rest for 2 minutes. To serve, spread jam on 8 individual serving plates and top each with a crépinette. Garnish with herbs.

Fish & Chips

One of the oldest pubs in the country is tucked away in the heart of Edgartown. Opened in 1742, The Newes from America is a British pub with deep New England roots. You can just picture the whaling captains of yore cooling off with frosty ales after months away at sea. It has all the hallmarks of a classic tavern: a roaring fireplace, flowing beers, and a menu of hearty chowders, pies, and fish and chips. The addition of local Offshore Amber Ale makes the batter light and crispy. The pub fries its chips, but this oven-baked home version delivers irresistibly crunchy wedges without the fuss. Pass the malt vinegar.

SERVES 4

Chips

4 medium russet potatoes

¼ cup olive oil

½ teaspoon kosher salt

½ teaspoon freshly ground black pepper

Batter

1 cup all-purpose flour

1 tablespoon garlic powder

1 tablespoon onion powder

1 teaspoon kosher salt

2 teaspoons paprika

1 teaspoon baking powder

1 cup beer, such as Offshore Amber Ale

Fish

4 (7-ounce) cod loin fillets

1 cup all-purpose flour

2 teaspoons kosher salt, plus more for finishing

1 tablespoon white pepper

1 tablespoon paprika

1 tablespoon garlic powder

1 tablespoon onion powder

Vegetable oil for frying

Make the chips: Preheat the oven to 450°F. Line a large baking sheet with parchment paper. Cut each potato into 8 wedges. Place the wedges in a large bowl of cold water. Soak for 30 minutes, then drain and thoroughly pat dry with kitchen towels. Put the potato wedges on the prepared baking sheet and toss with the oil, salt, and pepper. Roast, turning once, until crisp on the outside, 30 to 35 minutes.

Make the batter: While the potatoes are roasting, whisk the flour with the garlic and onion powders, salt, paprika, and baking powder in a large bowl. Add the beer in a thin stream, whisking constantly. Whisk until smooth, then add ½ cup water and whisk again. Set aside.

Make the fish: Pat the cod dry with paper towels. Whisk the flour with the 2 teaspoons salt, pepper, paprika, and garlic and onion powders in a shallow dish.

Line a baking sheet with paper towels and set aside. Fill a deep, wide pot with 5 inches oil and heat to 385°F (a cube of bread dropped into the oil will brown in 10 seconds).

Dredge a piece of cod in the seasoned flour, then dip it into the beer batter, coating thoroughly. Add the fish to the oil, dragging it in a back-and-forth motion as you slide it in to help prevent it from sticking to the bottom of the pot. Repeat with remaining fish, working in batches to avoid crowding the pot. When the fish turns golden brown, 6 to 8 minutes, remove with a strainer and drain briefly on the paper towels. Season with salt while hot. Serve fish and chips piping hot.

Fishermen's Oysters

MARTHA'S VINEYARD SPEARPOINT OYSTERS, CHILMARK

Jeremy Scheffer hands over a freshly shucked oyster on his boat in Menemsha. We clink shells in an oyster cheers before knocking back one of his Spearpoints, and then another, and another. The oysters are ice-cold, plump, briny, and sweet—a true island delicacy. It's an idyllic Vineyard afternoon, one you never want to end. Back at his home in Chilmark, he whips up these meaty broiled oysters. It's hard to beat a raw oyster, but if you really want to impress someone, try this.

Jeremy hails from the legendary Larsen fishing clan, who came from Norway in 1925 and settled on Martha's Vineyard (Aunt Betsy runs Larsen's Fish Market and Stan Larsen of Menemsha Fish Market is Jeremy's first cousin, once removed). Jeremy's father, Roy, was an oysterman, and in 2010, Jeremy started his oyster farm in the pristine waters of Katama Bay and Menemsha Pond, where he dedicated himself to sustainably producing the perfect oyster. He's been supplying the island's best restaurants and raw bars ever since. These oysters are a meal, not an appetizer.

MAKES 24 OYSTERS; SERVES 3 TO 4 PER PERSON OR UP TO 6 FOR A HUNGRY FISHERMAN.

4 tablespoons unsalted butter

3 tablespoons extra virgin olive oil

Leaves of 1 sprig rosemary, finely chopped

4 cloves garlic, minced

1 bunch scallions, finely chopped, whites and greens separated

¼ cup flat-leaf parsley leaves, finely chopped

24 shucked oysters

2 "fishermen's" handfuls (2 cups) baby spinach

8 ounces cod, very thinly sliced into 24 pieces

⅓ cup shredded Parmesan

Finely ground black pepper

Melt the butter in a small saucepan over low heat and add the olive oil, rosemary, garlic, and scallion whites. Sauté for 8 minutes. Add the parsley and sauté until the scallions have completely softened, about 2 additional minutes.

Place the oysters in an oyster pan or on a baking sheet. Spoon the buttery herb sauce over each oyster. Sauté the spinach in a small skillet over medium heat with a drop of water until wilted, 1 minute. Squeeze out the excess water from the spinach.

Place an oven rack on the third shelf from the top and preheat the broiler.

Drape a slice of cod over each oyster, then top with a little spinach. Sprinkle with the Parmesan and scallion greens, and season with black pepper. Broil until golden and bubbling, 7 to 8 minutes. Serve hot.

Grilled Swordfish
with Sungold Tomato Butter

S&S KITCHENETTE, VINEYARD HAVEN

There's something about Spring Sheldon, who is a world traveler, bon vivant, and community builder. S&S Kitchenette is her castle. The enchanting café-meets-salon might host a dance party one night, aura readings another. And the food is always magical. This swordfish dish is simple yet special; the golden butter should be a go-to for any gardener with a glut of candy-like Sungold tomatoes. Once you have a batch in your fridge, you'll find it also sings over grilled chicken or veggie kebabs. "So many people tell me, 'I never liked swordfish until I tried yours!'" laughs Spring. "It's a meaty fish, so just treat it like steak. High heat, sear on both sides, then remove from the heat and let it rest. It will continue to cook off the heat. Less is more—except with this butter, more is more!" The sweetness of Sungold tomatoes is perfect for this preparation, but other ripe cherry tomatoes will work, too.

SERVES 4

16 tablespoons
(2 sticks) unsalted
butter

8 ounces Sungold
tomatoes

Kosher salt

¼ cup olive oil

2 cloves garlic, minced

1 teaspoon finely
grated lemon zest

1 teaspoon freshly
ground black pepper

1 (1½-pound)
swordfish steak

Cilantro leaves
for garnish

Roasted red cherry
tomatoes for garnish

Watermelon radish,
cut into thin strips,
for garnish

Melt the butter in a small saucepan over medium heat. Add the tomatoes and simmer over low heat until the tomatoes burst, about 10 minutes. Allow to cool for 10 minutes. Blend the butter-tomato mixture in a blender on high speed until smooth and emulsified, about 2 minutes. Season with salt.

Combine the olive oil, garlic, lemon zest, and black pepper in a dish that fits the swordfish in a single layer. Add the fish, turn to coat, cover, and refrigerate for 1 to 2 hours.

Preheat a grill to high or heat a large cast-iron skillet over high heat. Remove the swordfish from the marinade and season with salt. Sear the fish without moving until browned, 5 to 7 minutes. It will detach from the grill grate or pan when it is ready. If it sticks, continue cooking until it releases. Turn and cook until browned on the other side, 5 to 7 additional minutes. Remove the fish from the heat and allow to rest for 5 minutes.

Pool the butter sauce on a platter and plate the fish on top. Garnish with cilantro, roasted tomatoes, and watermelon radish slices and serve family style.

Grilled Whole Fish
with Stir-Fried Vegetables, Fragrant Rice & Salsa Verde

THE PORT HUNTER, EDGARTOWN

"You won't find branzino or snapper on this menu," says The Port Hunter owner Patrick Courtney. Patrick and his brother, chef Ted Courtney, opened the restaurant as a place to hang after work and named it after a 1918 shipwreck. (The Covington, their sister restaurant across the street, is named for the tugboat with which it collided.) It's smooth sailing within, though, with a menu centered on island seafood. "The quality of food on the island is always inspiring," continues Patrick. "We have access to incredible products produced by great people." Fluke is a favorite to use due to its flaky texture and buttery flavor, but use whatever is local and fresh for you.

SERVES 2

Salsa Verde

3 cups flat-leaf parsley leaves

3 cups cilantro leaves

3 cups fresh oregano leaves

1 small shallot, chopped

1 clove garlic, chopped

1 small jalapeño, seeded

½ small red chili pepper, seeded

1 cup extra virgin olive oil

2 tablespoons orange juice

1 tablespoon red wine vinegar

1 tablespoon tamari

Fish

1 (1½- to 2-pound) whole fish, scaled, gutted, and gills removed

1 tablespoon extra virgin olive oil, plus more for pan

Kosher salt and freshly ground black pepper

Rice

2 tablespoons vegetable oil

1 tablespoon diced shallot

1 teaspoon freshly minced ginger

1 teaspoon kosher salt

1 cup jasmine rice, rinsed

Vegetables

¼ teaspoon chopped ginger

¼ teaspoon chopped garlic

3 tablespoons tamari

1 tablespoon lime juice

1 teaspoon toasted sesame oil

1 teaspoon mirin

1 teaspoon light brown sugar

2 tablespoons vegetable oil

1 small carrot, sliced into thin rounds

1 small yellow squash, sliced into half-moons

⅓ cup snap peas

⅓ large zucchini, cut into matchsticks

¼ small red onion, thinly sliced

¼ small red bell pepper, cut into matchsticks

2 shiitake mushrooms, stemmed and thinly sliced

5 basil leaves

Make the salsa verde: Combine the ingredients in a food processor fitted with the metal blade. Pulse until combined but not perfectly smooth. Set aside.

Make the fish: Preheat the oven to 425°F. Preheat a grill to medium. Lightly brush a baking sheet with olive oil. Make 3 shallow cuts on each side of the fish. Rub the 1 tablespoon olive oil on both sides of the fish, then season with salt and pepper.

With tongs, place the fish on the hottest part of the grill vertically to the grid and grill for 2 minutes, then rotate 90 degrees and grill for 2 additional minutes. Flip the fish and repeat. Remove the fish and place it on the prepared baking sheet. Place in the oven and roast until the flesh is flaky, 12 to 13 minutes for a 1½-pound fish and 16 to 17 minutes for a 2-pound fish.

Make the rice: Heat the vegetable oil in a medium saucepan over medium heat. Add the shallot, ginger, salt, and rice. Cook, stirring, for 2 minutes to toast the rice. Add 2 cups water, bring to a boil, and simmer for 5 minutes. Cover and cook over low heat until the water is fully absorbed and the rice is tender, 10 additional minutes.

Make the vegetables: In a small bowl, whisk together the ginger, garlic, tamari, lime juice, sesame oil, mirin, and sugar. Set aside. Heat the vegetable oil in a large skillet over medium-high heat. Add the vegetables and cook for 5 minutes, until crisp-tender. Remove from the heat and add the sauce. Toss the vegetables in the sauce, and if the sauce reduces too much from the residual heat, add 1 to 2 tablespoons water.

Serve the fish with the vegetables garnished with basil, and serve the rice and salsa verde alongside.

Jamaican Fried Chicken

VINEYARD CARIBBEAN CUISINE, OAK BLUFFS

Even on the wintriest day, Stacy Thomas's smile will make you feel like it's summer in Oak Bluffs. Behind the takeout window she runs with her husband, chef Newton Waite, Stacy greets all her customers like family, whether you're picking up a patty or need another shake of scotch bonnet sauce on your fried chicken. Newton's cooking is soul food, made with care; it is a taste of home. The fried chicken is the most popular dish, and for good reason. This is a golden-spiced, juicy bird that delivers all the island vibes. Naturally, serve with slaw, and rice and peas.

SERVES 4

2 cups whole milk

2 large eggs, beaten

1 tablespoon plus 1 teaspoon kosher salt

2 teaspoons Grace chicken seasoning

1 teaspoon ground ginger

8 pieces bone-in, skin-on chicken, such as thighs and drumsticks

Canola oil for frying

2 cups all-purpose flour

1½ teaspoons freshly ground black pepper

1½ teaspoons sweet paprika

1 teaspoon garlic powder

1 teaspoon onion salt

1 teaspoon dried oregano

1 teaspoon dried thyme

1 teaspoon ground white pepper

½ teaspoon Jamaican curry powder

Combine the milk, eggs, 1 teaspoon salt, chicken seasoning, and ground ginger in a large airtight container or large resealable bag. Place the chicken in the container, turn to coat, cover, and refrigerate for 8 hours.

Remove the chicken from the refrigerator 30 minutes before frying. Pour 1 inch of canola oil into a Dutch oven or other heavy pot with high sides. Heat to 325°F to 350°F over medium heat. (If you don't have a thermometer, stick the handle of a wooden spoon into the oil; if bubbles form around the wood, the oil is ready for frying. If it is bubbling hard, lower the heat and test again in a few minutes.)

Line a baking sheet with paper towels. Preheat the oven to 200°F. In a large bowl, combine the flour, remaining 1 tablespoon salt, black pepper, paprika, garlic powder, onion salt, oregano, thyme, white pepper, and curry powder. Working in batches to avoid crowding, dredge the chicken pieces in the seasoned flour and carefully place in the hot oil with tongs. Fry, turning once, until the chicken is deep golden brown and juices run clear when it is pierced in a thick spot, 16 to 18 minutes total. Remove each piece with tongs and drain briefly on the paper towels, then transfer to a baking sheet and keep warm while you fry the remaining chicken. Allow time for the oil to return to the proper temperature before proceeding with the next batch.

Jonah Crab Pasta

NANCY'S, OAK BLUFFS

Summer unofficially kicks off on Martha's Vineyard as soon as Nancy's reopens around Memorial Day. In a flash, the scents of fried fish, scallops, and clams tempt crowds to Oak Bluffs Harbor like a siren's song. Nancy's has been the quintessential hang since 1960, with celebrity guests and regulars stopping by for chowder, lobster rolls, and the signature Dirty Banana frozen cocktail. Upstairs, there's the boisterous joviality that you only find at an open-air bar by the water, where everyone is a few rum drinks in, yet the food is elevated beyond what you might expect from a place with a life-size shark jutting out of its facade. In addition to offering classic seafood fare, chef Alex Mueller likes to try new things: Nashville-style fried oysters might be a special one day, this luscious pasta with native Jonah crab another. Espelette is a mild pepper that brings citrusy warmth to the white wine butter sauce, and golden, garlicky breadcrumbs add a crown of crunch.

SERVES 4

1 pound spaghetti

Kosher salt

1 cup dry white wine

½ cup white wine vinegar

2 shallots, finely chopped

1½ sticks (12 tablespoons) cold unsalted butter, cubed

2 teaspoons Espelette pepper (or Aleppo pepper)

2 tablespoons chopped tarragon leaves

Freshly ground black pepper

2 tablespoons extra virgin olive oil

2 cloves garlic, minced

1 cup fresh breadcrumbs

1 pound cooked Jonah crabmeat, picked through for shells

Finely grated zest and juice of 1 small lemon

Minced fresh parsley, basil, and/or chives for garnish

Cook the spaghetti in a large pot of salted boiling water until al dente. Drain and set aside.

Combine the white wine, white wine vinegar, and shallots in a large, heavy-bottomed skillet. Bring to a simmer over medium heat then reduce the liquid by half, about 7 minutes.

Reduce the heat to low, and add the butter, a few cubes at a time, whisking until combined between additions and then cooking, still whisking, until the sauce is emulsified. Stir in the Espelette pepper and tarragon and season with salt and black pepper. Keep the sauce warm over low heat.

Heat the olive oil in a medium skillet over medium heat. Add the garlic and sauté until fragrant, 1 minute. Add the breadcrumbs and stir, cooking until golden brown and crispy, about 5 minutes. Season with salt and black pepper and set aside until ready to serve.

Add the drained spaghetti to the skillet with the white wine–butter sauce. Over low heat, gently fold in the crab and lemon zest and juice. Toss to combine and allow the crab to warm through in the sauce. Serve the pasta topped with the crispy breadcrumbs and garnished with herbs.

Lamb & Feta Meatballs

ALLEN FARM, CHILMARK

The oldest continuously working farm on Martha's Vineyard is also one of the most beautiful. Purchased in 1762 by Jonathan Allen, the Allen Farm has 100 acres of bucolic pastures and meadows overlooking the Atlantic that continue to be tended by the thirteenth generation of the same family. At the helm today are Clarissa; Mitchell; their son, Nathaniel; and his wife, Kaila. The farmstand is always worth a visit. There are homespun wool and woven keepsakes, and interesting cuts of lamb and mutton, like shanks and necks destined for low and slow cooking. What makes the meat so special is the way the animals are raised: organically and grass-fed, on fields infused with salt spray from the ocean, which seasons the meat similarly to the prized salt marsh lamb of Brittany and Wales.

Kaila is an instinctual cook with no formal training, yet she brings warmth and kindness to her table. On a bright October afternoon, she encouraged their children to join her in the kitchen, where they happily rolled out these simple, comforting lamb meatballs, dotted with creamy Mermaid Farm feta. Serve over greens or rice, dolloped with a yogurt and cucumber sauce.

MAKES SIXTEEN (1-INCH-DIAMETER) MEATBALLS; SERVES 4

1 pound ground lamb, such as Allen Farm

1 cup plain, whole milk yogurt, such as Mermaid Farm

½ cup feta, such as Mermaid Farm, crumbled

1 large egg, lightly beaten

½ cup fresh, dry, or panko breadcrumbs

1 teaspoon kosher salt

2 tablespoons unsalted butter or extra virgin olive oil

Mix the lamb, yogurt, feta, egg, breadcrumbs, and salt in a large bowl until well combined. With damp hands, roll the mixture into 1-inch balls.

Melt the butter in a large, heavy-bottomed skillet over medium-high heat. Working in batches to avoid crowding the pan (and using a splatter screen), cook meatballs until browned and crispy, 3 to 4 minutes, then turn the meatballs and brown until cooked through, 3 to 4 additional minutes. Transfer to a plate as they are cooked. Serve hot.

Lobster Gnocchi

Old-world elegance awaits at The Charlotte Inn. It feels as if you're stepping into another era as you're welcomed in The Terrace restaurant's fern-draped sunroom. Chef Zach Prifti produces food as picturesque as the inn. He focuses on local purveyors, such as The Net Result, that source fresh Menemsha lobster for this elegant entrée. "I thought of the flavors that visitors love to enjoy while vacationing on our little island in New England, while putting my French twist on this dish," says Zach. The base is a silky vegetable purée rather than a heavy cream sauce, making this perfect for date night at home.

SERVES 4

Gnocchi

⅓ cup whole milk ricotta

2 medium russet potatoes

1 large egg, lightly beaten

⅔ cup all-purpose flour

1½ teaspoons kosher salt, plus more for salting the pasta water

½ teaspoon freshly ground black pepper

½ teaspoon garlic powder

½ teaspoon onion powder

Cornmeal, for dusting

Extra virgin olive oil, for drizzling

Vegetable Purée

¼ cup extra virgin olive oil

½ cup chopped Spanish onion

1 large clove garlic, chopped

1 rib celery, chopped

½ cup chopped daikon radish

½ cup chopped peeled russet potato

½ cup chopped peeled sweet potato

¼ cup cubes peeled butternut squash

¼ cup chopped fennel bulb

6 cups vegetable broth

¼ cup heavy cream

3 tablespoons honey

2 tablespoons za'atar

1 tablespoon kosher salt

1½ teaspoons freshly ground black pepper

Lobster

8 tablespoons (1 stick) unsalted butter, cubed

1 tablespoon lemon juice

4 raw lobster tails, shelled

4 cooked lobster claws (optional)

1 tablespoon plus 1½ teaspoons extra virgin olive oil

4 button mushrooms, stemmed

½ leek, white part cut into matchsticks

1 large clove garlic, minced

¼ cup heavy cream

Kosher salt and freshly ground black pepper

Red sorrel leaves for garnish

Make the gnocchi: Set a strainer in a bowl. Wrap the ricotta in cheesecloth, place in the strainer, and weigh the ricotta down with a heavy bowl or jar. Refrigerate for 8 hours.

Preheat the oven to 450°F. Bake the potatoes on a baking sheet until a fork easily pierces the flesh, 45 to 60 minutes. Once the potatoes are cool enough to handle, peel and quarter them. Rice the potatoes onto a clean work surface and shape them into a well. Add the egg to the center of the well and crumble the drained ricotta over the top. Sift the flour over the potatoes, then add the salt, pepper, and garlic and onion powders. With your hands, lightly fold the ingredients together to form a dough, then gently knead until smooth, about 2 minutes.

Line a baking sheet with parchment paper and dust with cornmeal. Roll the dough into a 1½-foot-long log and divide into 3 equal pieces. Roll each piece into a 1-foot-long log about 1 inch in diameter and cut into 1½-inch pieces (you should have about 32 pieces). Roll each piece lightly over the back of a fork to create ridges. As you cut and shape the gnocchi, place them on the prepared baking sheet (make sure the gnocchi are not touching to prevent them from sticking together).

Line a baking sheet with parchment paper and set aside. Fill a large pot three-quarters of the way up the sides with water. Bring to a boil and season well with kosher salt. Prepare a bowl with ice water. Add the gnocchi to the boiling water, working in batches if necessary to avoid crowding. Boil until the gnocchi float to the top, 3 to 5 minutes. Using a slotted spoon, transfer the gnocchi to the ice bath, then use the slotted spoon to transfer the gnocchi from the ice bath to the prepared baking sheet. Drizzle lightly with olive oil. Repeat with the remaining gnocchi.

Make the vegetable purée: Wash the pot in which you cooked the gnocchi. Heat the olive oil in the pot over medium heat. Add the onion and garlic and sauté until softened, 3 minutes. Add the celery, daikon, potato, sweet potato, squash, and fennel and sauté for 5 minutes. Add the broth and bring to a boil. Lower the heat to medium-low and simmer until the vegetables are soft, about 45 minutes. Using a slotted spoon, transfer the vegetables to a blender. Add cooking liquid into the blender to cover the vegetables by three-quarters. Add the cream, honey, za'atar, salt, and pepper and blend on high speed until completely smooth, about 2 minutes. Set aside while you cook the lobster.

Make the lobster: Combine 7 tablespoons of the cubed butter, 1 cup water, and 1 teaspoon of the lemon juice in a large skillet over medium-low heat. When the butter begins to melt, add the lobster tails. Cook until the meat is no longer translucent, about 8 minutes, turning once. Add the lobster claw, if using, in the last 2 minutes to warm through. Remove and set aside.

Heat the olive oil in another large skillet and place over medium heat. Sauté the mushrooms, leek, and garlic until they start to soften, about 2 minutes. Add the gnocchi and sauté until the gnocchi turn golden brown, 5 to 7 minutes. Reduce the heat to medium-low. Add the cream and the remaining lemon juice. Season with salt and pepper. When the sauce begins to bubble, add the remaining 1 tablespoon butter and toss until the butter has melted and the sauce is velvety, about 2 minutes. Divide the vegetable purée evenly among 4 shallow bowls. Divide the gnocchi and lobster tails and claws, if using, among the bowls. Garnish with sorrel.

Moroccan Lamb Stew

SLOUGH FARM, EDGARTOWN

What are winters like on Martha's Vineyard? First-time visitors ask that question about as often as they ask where the nearest vineyard is (see page 10). Truth is, winter on the island is magical. It's a time to catch your breath, recharge, and enjoy short days with the fire on, a pot of stew made with tender, local lamb on the simmer, aromatic with sweet and warming spices.

This is a favorite winter recipe of Charlie Granquist, culinary director at Slough Farm in Katama. The sustainable, nonprofit farm with its iconic silo is a very special place that nourishes the community in abundance. Everything grown on the forty-five-acre farm is either donated through partnerships with Island Grown Initiative, the Island Food Pantry, and island schools, among others, or used in culinary programs that host visiting chefs and creatives from near and far. Winter welcomes the start of hands-on cooking classes with Charlie, who inspires kids and cooks of all levels on subjects from seasonal cooking to whole animal butchery. Summer visitors can arrange flowers picked from the garden to gift to patients of the local hospice before a yoga session at dusk.

A whisper of advice: Make the full recipe of this stew, regardless of whether you are cooking for one or many. The stew only gets more luscious as the days pass, and it freezes well. Couscous is a natural partner here.

SERVES 6 TO 8

¼ cup canola oil

5 pounds lamb shoulder (or stew meat), cut into 2-inch chunks

Kosher salt

1 small yellow onion, diced

2 carrots, diced

3 cloves garlic, peeled and crushed

1 (1-inch) piece ginger, peeled and crushed

3 tablespoons coriander seeds, toasted and ground

3 tablespoons ras el hanout

2 tablespoons cumin seeds, toasted

2 tablespoons turmeric

1 cinnamon stick

1 habanero pepper

1 (28-ounce) can whole peeled tomatoes, crushed by hand

5 cups chicken stock

2 (15-ounce) cans chickpeas, drained and rinsed

1½ cups dried apricots

1 medium winter squash, seeded and cut into 1-inch dice

Freshly ground black pepper

Yogurt and cilantro and mint leaves for garnish

Preheat the oven to 325°F. Heat the oil in a large Dutch oven with a lid over medium-high heat. Season the lamb with salt. Working in batches, brown the lamb pieces on all sides, about 8 minutes. With tongs, transfer the browned meat to a large plate.

Lower the heat to medium and sauté the onion, carrots, garlic, and ginger until the onions are soft and translucent, about 8 minutes. Add the coriander, ras el hanout, cumin, turmeric, and cinnamon. Cook until the spices are fragrant, 1 to 2 minutes. Add the habanero, crushed tomatoes, chicken stock, and chickpeas. Return the lamb and any juices to the pot and bring to a simmer. Cover the pot, place it in the oven, and cook for 2 hours.

After 2 hours, add the dried apricots and squash, then cover and return the pot to the oven for 1 additional hour. The lamb should be tender and pierce easily with a fork. Season with salt and pepper.

To serve, remove and discard the cinnamon stick. Transfer the stew to individual serving bowls and top with yogurt and herbs.

Old Bay–Crusted Black Sea Bass
with Corn Sauce & Summer Succotash

LAMBERT'S COVE INN, WEST TISBURY

Lambert's Cove Inn is a boutique hideaway that welcomes guests with all the quiet luxuries—and alpacas. The sweet, fuzzy residents only add to the charm. A love of nature brought innkeepers Galen and Bridget Sampson to the converted 1790 farmhouse. "Every day, we are grateful that we can walk out our door and experience the sea, the farms, and the towns of our island," says Galen. "It is such a warm and special place with tremendous diversity and heart." This is a dish that represents Galen's love of local ingredients. Herbs come from the garden that Bridget manages. The sea bass arrives fresh off the Menemsha docks from the MV Seafood Collaborative, a nonprofit that supports local independent commercial fishermen and aquaculture farmers. "It is so important to us to help the island's fishing history and traditions survive," says Galen. "We do our small part by featuring the fishermen's delicious products on our menu and advocating to our guests to do the same in their kitchens."

SERVES 4

Sauce

1 tablespoon extra virgin olive oil

3 tablespoons minced shallots

1¾ cups fresh corn kernels

1 bay leaf

½ teaspoon thyme leaves

2 tablespoons white wine

¼ cup heavy cream

Kosher salt and freshly ground white pepper

Succotash

2 tablespoons extra virgin olive oil

1 cup finely diced yellow onion

1 cup finely diced zucchini

1 cup finely diced red bell pepper

Kernels from 4 ears corn (about 3 cups); see corn-shaving instructions, page 120

1 jalapeño, seeded and minced

¼ cup minced flat-leaf parsley leaves

3 tablespoons thinly sliced basil

Kosher salt and coarsely ground black pepper

Fish

1 cup medium-grind cornmeal

2 tablespoons Old Bay seasoning

½ teaspoon freshly ground black pepper

2 tablespoons vegetable oil, or more as needed

4 (6-ounce) skin-on black sea bass fillets

Edible flowers for garnish

Make the sauce: Heat the oil in a medium saucepan over medium heat. Sauté the shallot, stirring frequently, until translucent but not browned, about 4 minutes. Add the corn, bay leaf, and thyme and sauté until fragrant, 3 minutes. Add the wine and cook, stirring, for 1 minute. Add the cream, bring to a boil, reduce the heat to medium-low, and simmer for 5 to 7 minutes to thicken slightly. Allow to cool, then remove and discard the bay leaf and use an immersion blender to blend until smooth and spreadable, thinning with water if necessary. Season with salt and white pepper. Set aside and keep warm.

Make the succotash: Preheat the oven to 200°F. Heat 1 tablespoon of the oil in a large, ovenproof skillet over medium heat. Sauté the onion until translucent, about 7 minutes. Add the remaining 1 tablespoon oil, then the zucchini and bell pepper, and sauté until starting to soften, 5 minutes. Add the corn and sauté until the corn is crisp-tender, about 3 minutes. Remove from the heat and allow to cool. Add the jalapeño, parsley, and basil. Season with salt and black pepper. Keep warm in the oven while you cook the fish.

Make the fish: Whisk the cornmeal, Old Bay, and black pepper together on a baking sheet.

Heat the oil in a large, heavy-bottomed skillet over medium heat. When the oil is shimmering, dredge the fish in the cornmeal mixture. Shake off any excess and set as many fillets as will fit in a single layer without crowding in the skillet. Cook until golden brown, 2 to 3 minutes, then turn and cook until golden brown on the other side, 2 to 3 additional minutes. Keep the cooked fillets warm on a baking sheet in the oven while you cook the rest, adding more oil to the skillet as needed. To plate, smear corn sauce on the bottom of 4 individual plates. Spoon succotash over the top, and place 1 fish fillet over the vegetables. Garnish with edible flowers and serve.

Orecchiette with Lamb Ragù

MARTHA'S VINEYARD PASTA, WEST TISBURY

When the delightful Katie Leaird began selling her homemade pasta, the island breathed a collective sigh of relief. Previously, fresh pasta was almost impossible to find, so, Katie to the rescue! Katie's career has been dedicated to the culinary arts, including cooking at a Michelin-starred restaurant in Italy. While you can pair this silky ragù with whichever shape is your favorite, orecchiette cups the sauce beautifully. Plus, this pasta is fun to make, especially with little ones, who can easily flip the pasta rounds over their thumbs to achieve the ear shape. The fried sage leaves add crunch to the finished dish. To make them, heat a couple tablespoons of olive oil in a small skillet. Add the leaves in a single layer and fry for 30 seconds. Drain on paper towels as you prepare the pasta.

SERVES 4 TO 6

1½ pounds bone-in lamb loin or shoulder chops

Kosher salt and freshly ground black pepper

¼ cup plus 2 teaspoons extra virgin olive oil

2 cups dry white wine

2½ cups chicken broth

3 cloves garlic, peeled and crushed

1 sprig rosemary

1 sprig sage

2 cups double-milled semolina flour, plus more for dusting

2 ribs celery, diced

1 medium onion, finely chopped

1 carrot, diced

½ bulb fennel, cored and diced

2 tablespoons tomato paste

4 cloves garlic, minced

2 tablespoons finely chopped fresh sage leaves

1 tablespoon finely chopped fresh rosemary leaves

½ cup frozen peas

12 fried sage leaves (see method, above)

Grated Pecorino Romano for serving

Season the lamb with salt and pepper. Heat 2 tablespoons olive oil in a Dutch oven over medium-high heat until shimmering. Brown the lamb on one side, about 5 minutes. Turn and continue to cook until browned on the other side, 5 minutes more.

Add 1 cup wine and use a wooden spoon to scrape up any browned bits from the bottom of the pot. Cook until the liquid is slightly reduced, about 2 minutes. Add 1 cup chicken broth, the garlic, and rosemary and sage sprigs. Reduce the heat to medium-low and cook, covered, until the meat is falling off the bone, about 1 hour.

Let the lamb cool, then pick the meat off and shred it into bite-size pieces by hand. Discard the garlic, rosemary, sage, and bones. Toss the lamb with any remaining cooking liquid, then transfer to a bowl, cover, and refrigerate.

To make the pasta dough, place the 2 cups semolina flour in a large bowl. Add ⅔ cup room temperature water and the 2 teaspoons olive oil and use a fork to mix everything together to form a shaggy dough. Transfer the dough to a clean work surface and knead by hand until smooth, 3 to 5 minutes. Cover the dough with a kitchen towel and let it rest for 1 hour.

Roll a small portion of the dough into a rope about ¾ inch in diameter. Cut the rope into ½-inch pieces. Use a butter knife to scrape each piece of dough to flatten. Then, one at a time, shape each piece over your thumb. Set aside on a baking sheet dusted with semolina flour. Continue with the remaining dough.

To make the ragù, heat the remaining 2 tablespoons olive oil in a Dutch oven over medium heat. Sauté the celery, onion, carrot, and fennel until softened, about 8 minutes. Add the tomato paste and garlic and cook, stirring, until fragrant, about 2 additional minutes. Add the remaining 1 cup wine and use a wooden spoon to scrape up any browned bits from the bottom of the pot. Cook until just slightly reduced, about 2 minutes.

Add the remaining 1½ cups chicken broth and chopped sage and rosemary leaves. Bring the mixture to a simmer, then reduce the heat to medium-low and simmer, covered, for 30 minutes. Uncover, stir in the lamb, and cook until thickened, about 15 minutes.

Bring a large pot of water to a boil. Salt the water, add the orecchiette, and cook until the pasta floats to the surface and is cooked through, about 3 minutes. Reserve 1 cup of the pasta cooking water and drain. Toss the cooked pasta with the lamb ragù. Stir in the peas and season with salt and pepper. Thin with a bit of reserved cooking water, if necessary. Serve with the fried sage leaves and Pecorino.

Pizza
with Potatoes, Leek Cream & Bacon

STONEY HILL PIZZA, WEST TISBURY

Consider this your pizza master class. Nina Levin is the island's *pizzaiola*, baking pies in her cute-as-a-pie red-and-white-tiled mobile wood-fired pizza oven. Born and raised on Martha's Vineyard, she worked as a chef around the country before coming home and building the oven herself. She quickly gained a reputation for making showstopping pizzas with unique toppings (here's looking at you, corn and shiitakes). The sourdough starter used to leaven the dough creates complex flavor with a wonderful tang. So, take this as your sign to throw a pizza party. Use Nina's dough as your springboard for seasonal flavors. Burrata and cherry tomatoes are summer's best friends, and when the temperatures fall, can you imagine a better combo than meltingly silky leeks, potato, smoky bacon, and nutty Fontina cheese? This recipe gives weight in grams for precision, so use a scale for measuring (and because it's easier to weigh everything in one bowl). The sourdough process takes a few days, so plan ahead (it's worth it!). Or use your favorite yeast pizza dough recipe and follow with the toppings suggested here.

MAKES THREE (14-INCH) PIZZAS

Day 1: Levain

8 g whole wheat flour

250 g bread flour

260 g room temperature water

52 g active sourdough starter

Days 2 and 3: Dough

560 g bread flour

375 g room temperature water

100 g levain

15 g kosher salt

Olive oil for coating

All-purpose flour for work surface

Day 4: Pizzas

8 ounces bacon, diced

4 tablespoons unsalted butter

5 leeks (white and light green parts only), cut into thin strips, rinsed, and drained

Kosher salt and freshly ground black pepper

2 cups heavy cream

1 large potato, thinly sliced

½ cup rice flour (or all-purpose flour)

½ cup bread flour

½ cup semolina flour

1 pound Fontina, cut into ½-inch dice

1 tablespoon chopped rosemary leaves

1 tablespoon chopped thyme leaves

1 tablespoon chopped flat-leaf parsley leaves

Extra virgin olive oil for drizzling

Day 1

Make the levain: Mix the wheat and bread flours, water, and sourdough starter in a medium bowl. Cover and store in a warm part of your kitchen. If your home is cold, store in the oven with the light on. Allow to rest for 12 hours.

Day 2

Make the dough: In a stand mixer fitted with the dough hook, mix the bread flour and water on low speed until there are no signs of dry flour, about 5 minutes. Allow to rest for 30 minutes.

Add 100 g of the levain to the dough and mix on low until incorporated. Sprinkle the salt in while the mixer is running.

Oil a large bowl, then turn the dough out into the bowl and cover with a kitchen towel. Allow to rest for 3 hours.

RECIPE CONTINUES

Fold the dough using the stretch and fold method (see page 45) every hour for 3 hours. Once you've finished folding, cover the dough and refrigerate for at least 8 hours.

Day 3

Lightly coat a large baking sheet with olive oil. Lightly flour a work surface. Turn the dough out and sprinkle with a little more flour. Using a knife or a bench scraper, cut the dough into three equal pieces.

Working with one piece of dough at a time, gently lift the dough and allow the edges to fold and tuck underneath. Use a bench scraper to tuck the edges in while turning the dough in a circle, creating tension with each turn until the dough is smooth on top and forms a tight ball. Keep covered while you repeat with the remaining pieces.

Using your bench scraper or your hands, place the pieces of dough onto the oiled baking sheet. Cover with a damp kitchen towel and allow to rest at room temperature for 1 hour. After 1 hour, refrigerate overnight, still covered with a damp kitchen towel.

Day 4

Make the pizzas: Combine the bacon with ¼ cup water in a medium skillet over medium-low heat and cook until the bacon is crisp and the water has evaporated, 10 to 12 minutes. Once the bacon is crisp, strain it through a fine-mesh sieve (reserve bacon grease for another use). Drain the bacon on a plate lined with paper towels.

Return the skillet to low heat and melt the butter. Add the leeks and season with salt and pepper. (Keep in mind that the bacon may be salty.) Cook, stirring frequently, until soft and translucent, 25 to 30 minutes. Add a splash of water if the leeks begin to brown. Taste and adjust seasoning. Add the cream and simmer until thickened, 10 to 15 minutes. Taste and adjust seasoning. Transfer the leek cream mixture to a bowl and cool to room temperature before using.

Soak the potato slices in a bowl of lukewarm water with a generous amount of salt for 30 minutes. Drain and pat dry with paper towels.

Now it's time to start making the pizzas! Remove the dough from the refrigerator and allow it to come to room temperature. Position an oven rack at the lowest level with a pizza stone and heat to 500°F for 30 minutes. (If you have a pizza oven, heat according to the instructions.)

Mix the rice and bread flours in a small bowl. Sprinkle a wooden pizza peel or large wooden cutting board with a generous dusting of the semolina flour.

While the oven is preheating, start stretching the dough. Place one ball of dough smooth side up on a heavily floured surface (keep the other dough balls covered with a kitchen towel). Sprinkle the top of the dough generously with the rice and bread flour mixture and begin shaping the dough, being sure to keep the smooth side facing up. Shape the crust by gently pressing down ¼ to ½ inch from the outside of the dough to preserve a raised rim. Once you've made a rim all the way around, pick up the dough and continue to follow the outline of your outer crust using gravity to stretch it out until it is about 14 inches in diameter.

Gently place the dough, smooth side up, on the prepared pizza peel.

Top with one-third each of the leek cream mixture, potatoes, Fontina, and bacon. Gently move the pizza back and forth on the peel to make sure it isn't sticking. If the pizza sticks, gently lift it up and slide some more semolina flour underneath until the pizza moves freely on the peel.

Carefully slide your pizza off the peel onto the hot baking stone. The key is confidence! Immediately turn the oven down to 450°F and bake for 6 minutes. Check for doneness by gently lifting up the pizza and checking for browning on the bottom; it should hold its shape with no sag and be lightly browned. If needed, bake for an additional 2 to 3 minutes.

With a metal pizza peel or large spatula, transfer the pizza to a wire cooling rack. Sprinkle with one-third of the herbs. Drizzle with extra virgin olive oil. Repeat with the remaining dough and toppings.

Roast Chicken of Dreams
with Cherry Tomatoes & Crispy Shiitakes

NORTH TABOR FARM, CHILMARK

"Our winters are long," says North Tabor Farm owner Rebecca Miller over supper on the farm. "Breaking bread together is how we survive." That solidarity with the community defines Rebecca and her husband, Matthew Dix, who started the six-acre farm in 1994. Dogs, chickens, and pigs rule the farm that is today managed by their youngest daughter, Ruby. The farm is known for its pasture-raised, organically fed chickens, and the difference in flavor between those and most supermarket poultry is remarkable. "Good chickens are not cheap," says Matthew. "We are long overdue a reevaluation of industrial farming, subsidies, and the true price of food." Indeed, tasting a North Tabor Farm chicken makes you value the hard work and dedication of small-scale farmers. The farm produces about forty chickens a week, and if you're lucky enough to be driving past and see the FRESH CHICKEN sign on North Road, take it as a hint to make this perfect roast chicken. If you're off-island, seek out the best chicken you can.

On the day we visited, Gina Citarella, who often helms the farm kitchen, served this golden chicken with puffy sourdough focaccia (an essential mop for those jammy, lemony juices), roast potatoes, and Rebecca's favorite accompaniment, the farm's signature Peace Greens dressed in nothing more than good olive oil.

SERVES 4

Kosher salt

1 (3½- to 4-pound) whole chicken

1 pound cherry tomatoes

1 pound shiitake mushrooms

5 cloves garlic

3 tablespoons tarragon leaves

3 tablespoons thyme leaves

Extra virgin olive oil for roasting

1 small yellow onion, quartered

1 lemon, zested and halved

Salt the chicken liberally and refrigerate on a plate, uncovered, for up to 24 hours (see Note). Remove the chicken 30 minutes before cooking and allow it to sit at room temperature.

Preheat the oven to 425°F. Position a rack in the center and a rack in the lower third. Place the cherry tomatoes, half of the mushrooms, 3 cloves garlic, half of the tarragon, and half of the thyme in a 10-inch cast-iron skillet. Season with salt and toss with a generous amount of olive oil.

Stuff the chicken with the remaining 2 cloves garlic, the onion, the lemon halves, and the remaining tarragon and thyme. Arrange the chicken on top of the tomato-shiitake mix in the cast-iron skillet.

In an 8-inch cast-iron skillet, toss the remaining shiitakes with a generous amount of olive oil and season with salt. Place the pan with the chicken onto the center rack and place the pan with the shiitakes on the lower rack.

Roast until the mushrooms are crisp, about 15 minutes. Remove the mushrooms and lower the heat to 375°F. After 30 minutes, rotate the 10-inch pan 180 degrees. Roast until the chicken is golden brown, juices run clear when you insert a knife in the thickest part of the thigh, and an instant-read thermometer reads 165°F, 30 to 40 additional minutes.

Let the chicken rest at room temperature for 10 to 15 minutes. Warm the crispy shiitakes in the oven while the chicken is resting. Carve the chicken and serve with the tomato-shiitake pan sauce, top with the crispy shiitakes, and finish with the lemon zest.

Note: Salting and chilling the chicken, uncovered in the fridge for up to 1 day before roasting, seasons the chicken all the way through and ensures that the skin will be crispy.

Quick Chicken Stock: A chicken this special deserves to be used without any waste, so salvage the carcass, along with other veggie and herb scraps, add to a large pot, fill with water, salt the water, place over medium-low heat, skim the froth from time to time, and you'll have a golden homemade chicken stock in about 1 hour.

Liz Ragone

Liz Ragone overflows with creativity. She grew up on the Cape, and studied fashion design in San Francisco. Since coming to Martha's Vineyard, Liz has focused on botanical stained-glass arts, inspired by the nature around her. She's known for hosting Sunday suppers, gathering loved ones for a feast of food and friendship on the farm.

My perfect Vineyard day unfolds organically and requires no planning. It may start early in the lavender labyrinth with a homegrown lavender latte made with Chilmark Coffee Company espresso. While I'm down there, I harvest more lavender for evening cocktails, then over to the hoop house to pick tulsi, aka holy basil, lemon balm, lemon verbena, and mint. I fill a carafe with the herbs and water and let the sun do its work. This "sun tea" will be perfect for a mood-boosting afternoon pick-me-up. Now that I'm fully caffeinated, I fill a basket of edible flowers and head back to the house. This confetti of edibles usually includes pansies, violas, marigolds, calendula, scarlet runner, and hyacinth bean flowers, and my favorite, bachelor buttons.

The days are busy and long during summer. There's a palpable energy in the air that's undeniable. In the year-round community, we share an understanding that these days are fleeting and we must revel in every moment.

By noon, the flowers and veggies are harvested. Private chefs and caterers have picked up their bounty. A flower arrangement is sent off with Nina Levin of Stoney Hill Pizza and several containers of edible flowers are en route to a wedding in Leila Gardner's Cocktail Caravan.

Usually at around three p.m., just as I'm craving a snack, J. P. Shepard stops by from his blacksmith shop with a bag of Signature oysters and a cooler of cold PBRs. Nothing beats this combo after a long day in the sun—except maybe that homegrown sun tea, which is usually ready by this time.

Before you know it, the long rustic farm tables are being dragged out and someone is heading down to the storage shed to fill the tractor with an assortment of thrifted antique cane chairs to seat hungry guests.

Anyone who frequents Sunday supper knows what to do when they arrive. Everyone immediately lends a hand. The eclectic mix of glassware needs to be set near the buckets of donated wine. The mix-and-match cloth napkins and cutlery are arranged. There are always flower enthusiasts who jump at the opportunity to harvest strawflowers, celosia, gomphrena, and other everlasting flowers for the repurposed bud vases. (I'll turn these flowers into flower crowns for the farmers market the following Wednesday.)

By dark, the scene has been set. The string lights around the garden and tables are lit. Votive candles in vintage bottles twinkle. The grill is hot. Scents of whole smoked local fish and homemade lamb sausages from The Swimming Pig's Tyler Potter waft in the air. The kitchen is bustling with helping hands and inspired chefs. Just as we realize that we forgot to prep a salad, Ruby Dix, Kyle Bullerjahn, and Gina Citarella of North Tabor Farm show up with bags of the freshest Peace Greens. That edible flower confetti is sprinkled everywhere, and the buffet table is now overflowing with offerings from our guests. Lexie Roth and Eva Faber from Goldie's Rotisserie have brought their famous roast chickens and soba noodles.

The effortless dance that is Sunday supper is such a beautiful thing to witness. Drinks are cheered, laughter is shared, not a morsel of food is wasted, instruments are played, songs are sung, and when it's all over, everyone asks, "Same time next week?"

Seared Scallops
with Lemon Mustard Sauce & Ginger Pea Purée

THE CHAPPY KITCHEN, EDGARTOWN

"I adored Uncle Neil," says The Chappy Kitchen owner, Katie Kidder, speaking of her godfather. "He loved life, loved his family, and loved this mustard." The Vineyard's favorite condiment began life as a secret recipe, given to Neil by a client. He bottled it for gifts and always kept a jar in his fridge. Today, it's proudly served on fine dining menus, including those of Alchemy and The Terrace, and it's part of The Chappy Kitchen's popular summer catering offerings. In addition to serving the Dijon-style mustard alongside fresh pretzels for dunking, Katie uses it to make a piquant sauce to drizzle over plump local scallops, whose sweetness plays beautifully against a warming ginger pea purée. An impressive dinner party dish if ever there was one. "The FV Martha Rose in Menemsha harvests the most delicious scallops," says Katie. "I love to buy them from The Fish House and support our local fishermen. The same goes for our fabulous farms: Morning Glory and The Grey Barn, and Slip Away on Chappy help our mission of being as farm-to-table as possible."

SERVES 6

Ginger Pea Purée

2 cups shelled peas

Kosher salt

1 large clove garlic, roughly chopped

1 (1-inch) piece ginger, peeled and chopped

2 tablespoons extra virgin olive oil

2 tablespoons lemon juice

Freshly ground black pepper

Scallops

24 large sea scallops, patted dry

Kosher salt and freshly ground black pepper

4 tablespoons unsalted butter

2 tablespoons extra virgin olive oil

1 large clove garlic, crushed

2 cups dry white wine

¼ cup to ½ cup Dijon mustard, such as Uncle Neil's (or substitute ¼ cup Dijon and ¼ cup honey mustard)

¼ cup mascarpone or full-fat sour cream

Lemon juice for finishing

Microgreens and halved cherry tomatoes for garnish

Make the pea purée: Prepare a bowl of ice water. In a medium saucepan, bring 3 cups water to a boil. Add the peas and a large pinch of salt. Cook until the peas are tender, about 3 minutes. Reserve 1 cup of the cooking water, then drain the peas and transfer to the ice water. Drain the peas again. Set aside 2 tablespoons peas for garnish.

Combine the remaining peas, ¼ cup of the reserved water, garlic, ginger, olive oil, and lemon juice in a food processor fitted with the metal blade. Season with salt and pepper and process until smooth. Add more cooking water in small amounts to achieve a thick and creamy consistency. Taste and adjust seasoning. Transfer the pea purée to a bowl and cover to keep warm. You can make the purée 1 day ahead and reheat it in the top of a double boiler.

Make the scallops: Season the scallops on both sides with salt and pepper. Heat 2 tablespoons of the butter and the olive oil in a large, heavy-bottomed skillet large enough to hold 12 scallops in a single layer. Place over medium-high heat. Add 12 scallops and cook without moving until browned on the bottoms, about 1 minute, then flip and cook for 1 additional minute on the other side. Transfer to a plate. Repeat with the remaining scallops.

Scrape the browned bits off the bottom of the pan and add the garlic and remaining 2 tablespoons butter. Cook, stirring, for 1 minute. Add the white wine, ¼ cup mustard, ½ teaspoon salt, and ¼ teaspoon pepper. Whisk all the ingredients and simmer until the sauce has reduced by half, about 6 minutes. Taste and add more mustard if desired. Whisk in the mascarpone, then return the scallops to the skillet. Spoon the sauce over the scallops so they absorb some of the sauce, being careful not to overcook.

Spread the pea purée on 6 individual serving plates and place 4 scallops on each plate. Spoon additional mustard sauce over the scallops, and finish with lemon juice and garnishes.

Shrimp Aliyyeh

STATE ROAD, WEST TISBURY

From little things, big things grow. That's certainly the case with State Road, from its humble origins as a tiny 1950s vegetable shack and ice cream parlor to its present status as the beacon of casually chic mid-island dining. It's not hard to see why: Flowers and fairy lights welcome during summer; a roaring fire beckons over the winter. Then there's the menu of new American classics, with ingredients that owners Mary and Jackson Kenworth and chef Jonathan Warnock are proud to source locally. This is a dish that is much loved by Jonathan. Aliyyeh, a vivid Lebanese cilantro pesto fragrant with cinnamon (let's just say it gives basil pesto a run for its money), coats grilled or sautéed shrimp. In case some famous guests have snagged your table, enjoy this as an elegant weekend lunch or light dinner.

SERVES 4

Aliyyeh

¼ cup plus
2 tablespoons extra
virgin olive oil

2 tablespoons
plus 1½ teaspoons
minced garlic

¼ teaspoon kosher salt

¼ teaspoon ground
cinnamon

¼ teaspoon ground
cayenne pepper

⅛ teaspoon ground
turmeric

⅛ teaspoon freshly
ground black pepper

1 large bunch cilantro,
ends trimmed

Shrimp

Olive oil for grate
or sauteing

1 pound large shrimp,
peeled, deveined,
and patted dry

1 teaspoon kosher salt

Vinaigrette

½ cup canola oil

2 tablespoons white
wine vinegar

1 tablespoon fresh
lemon juice

1½ teaspoons
Dijon mustard

1 teaspoon honey

Good pinch kosher salt

Salad

4 cups arugula

½ fennel bulb, cored
and thinly sliced

12 kumquats, halved
and seeded

Make the aliyyeh: Gently warm the olive oil, garlic, and salt in a small saucepan over low heat until the garlic is soft, about 8 minutes. Remove from the heat and stir in the cinnamon, cayenne, turmeric, and black pepper. Cool completely, then transfer to a large bowl. Create a tight bundle of the cilantro and slice into a chiffonade (do not chop or use a food processor as it will bruise and darken the cilantro). Fold the cilantro into the sauce.

Make the shrimp: To grill the shrimp, preheat a grill to medium-high and lightly oil the grate. Season the shrimp with the salt. Grill the shrimp for 1 to 2 minutes on each side. (Alternatively, to sauté the shrimp, heat a little olive oil in a large skillet over medium-high heat. Season the shrimp with salt and sauté, working in batches to avoid crowding the pan, until opaque, 1 to 2 minutes per side.) Transfer the grilled or sautéed shrimp to the bowl with the aliyyeh and toss to coat.

Make the vinaigrette: In a blender, combine the oil, vinegar, lemon juice, mustard, honey, and salt until emulsified.

Make the salad: Toss the arugula with the fennel and kumquats in a medium bowl. Dress the salad with the vinaigrette. To serve, divide the salad among 4 individual serving plates and top with the shrimp.

Spaghetti & Cheesy Meatballs with Marinara

GOLDIE'S ROTISSERIE, CHILMARK

In 2021, a sunny food truck aptly named Goldie's Rotisserie lit up the island. Owners Eva Faber and Lexie Roth radiate a brilliant aura while slinging some of the best truck fare anywhere. Wherever they pull up, there's a line hungry for French onion hot dogs, rotisserie chicken, and shmaltz-licked potatoes; cooking that is intentional and supremely delicious.

Just like these meatballs and marinara. "Italian food is a shared love language of mine and Lexie's via our mothers, Gretchen and Deborah," says Eva. While the recipe is classic, there are some pro moves that elevate it to iconic. "For the meatballs, we use quality breadcrumbs made from real bread. Our meat comes from The Grey Barn, and a mix of beef, pork, and veal is the holy trifecta, making the most decadent meatball ever. All beef is just not as melty and good." Speaking of melty, you'll notice there's a hefty dose of Parmesan in the meatballs. "It's more Parm than you'd think," confirms Eva. "After you bake the balls there's a lot of cheese oozing out, but scrape all of that good stuff into your pot of sauce and keep simmering." Make this batch o' balls and use leftovers for the best meatball subs. This recipe is dedicated to all our mothers.

MAKES THIRTY (1½-INCH-DIAMETER) MEATBALLS; SERVES 6 TO 8

Marinara

½ cup extra virgin olive oil

1 medium yellow onion, diced

4 cloves garlic, thinly sliced

1 carrot, grated

¼ teaspoon crushed red pepper flakes, or more to taste

2 (28-ounce) cans whole peeled San Marzano tomatoes

Kosher salt and freshly ground black pepper

Meatballs

1 pound ground beef

½ pound ground pork

½ pound ground veal

1½ cups fresh breadcrumbs (see Note)

3 large eggs, lightly beaten

⅓ cup flat-leaf parsley leaves, finely chopped

1 cup grated Parmesan

1 to 2 teaspoons kosher salt

Freshly ground black pepper

1 to 2 tablespoons whole milk, if needed

Cooked spaghetti for serving

Whole basil leaves for serving

Make the marinara: Heat the olive oil in a large pot over medium heat. Add the onion and garlic and cook until very soft but not browned, 7 to 8 minutes. Add the carrot and pepper flakes and cook 5 additional minutes. Add the tomatoes with their juice and bring to a simmer. Reduce the heat to low and simmer, uncovered, stirring occasionally and breaking up the tomatoes with the back of a spoon, until the sauce thickens, about 1 hour. Season with salt and pepper. Purée with an immersion blender if you prefer a smooth sauce, or leave chunky. Set aside until ready to use.

Make the meatballs: Preheat the oven to 425°F and place a rack in the center. Combine the beef, pork, and veal, breadcrumbs, eggs, parsley, Parmesan, 1 teaspoon salt, and pepper to taste in a large bowl and mix together with clean hands. Don't compress too much—the mixture should be fairly soft, wet, and sticky; add milk 1 teaspoon at a time, if necessary, to achieve this consistency. Test the seasoning by cooking a small piece in a frying pan. Add more salt to the mix, if needed. Rest the mixture for at least 10 minutes or refrigerate up to 2 hours.

Wet your hands lightly and shape the meatballs into 1½-inch balls. Place the meatballs on a baking sheet lined with parchment paper; space them at least 1 inch apart. Place the sheet on the center rack and bake for 5 minutes. Flip the meatballs and bake until they are beginning to brown but not cooked through, 5 to 10 additional minutes. The meatballs will continue to cook in the sauce.

Remove the meatballs from the oven and place in the marinara. Cover and simmer until the meatballs are cooked through, at least 30 minutes. Serve with spaghetti and fresh basil.

Note: For the breadcrumbs, use a whole loaf of fresh, crusty artisan bread. Cut into cubes, place in a food processor fitted with the steel blade, pulse several times until half are very fine crumbs and half are larger, pea-size crumbs. Store extra breadcrumbs in a freezer-safe airtight container.

Stovetop Lobster Clambake

KATAMA GENERAL STORE, EDGARTOWN

You might pop in for a sandwich or hostess gift, but Katama General Store entices you to linger. It's the quintessential neighborhood bodega on the way to the beach, charmingly cavernous with all the Martha's Vineyard must-haves: beach towels and sand buckets, lobster rolls and pét-nats. Snacks for days. And then there's the wraparound porch, surely one of the prettiest on the island, inviting you to kick back with an iced coffee (or lean in for gossip).

No New England summer is complete without a clambake. The delightful owners, Jackie and Doug Korell, are known for traditional clambake cookouts on the beach. As embers glow against the sunset, they masterfully maneuver fire and smoke to create an unforgettable feast of the finest local shellfish and summer corn. Finger-licking, bib-wearing fun. And if the beach is out of reach, these bakemasters have perfected a stovetop method that delivers seaside satisfaction to your kitchen in under 30 minutes.

SERVES 4

1½ pounds red bliss creamer potatoes, par-cooked for 5 minutes

2 linguiça sausages, cut into 1-inch slices on the diagonal (optional)

4 ears corn, shucked

4 (1¼-pound) live lobsters

1 pound littleneck clams, cleaned

1 pound mussels, cleaned

2 large handfuls rockweed (optional)

Put 2 cups water in a 12-quart stockpot with tight-fitting lid. Place the ingredients in the stockpot in the following order: potatoes on the bottom, then linguiça, if using, followed by corn, lobsters, clams, mussels, and rockweed, if using. Cover and bring to a boil over high heat. When you see steam, set your timer for 15 minutes.

Check the lobsters for doneness by gently twisting an antenna; it should remove easily. Discard any mussels or clams that haven't opened. Serve immediately.

Stuffed Lobster

LARSEN'S FISH MARKET, CHILMARK

Summer on the Vineyard isn't quite as magical without a visit to Larsen's Fish Market in Menemsha. The lobster dinners are legendary, with sunset seekers pitching their beach chairs and donning bibs along the shore. But diners also come for owner Betsy Larsen's megawatt smile, greeting regulars with the warmth of family. And it's all about family at Larsen's. Established in 1969 by her parents, Louis and Mary, Betsy started helping out at the fish market when she was fourteen, and was joined by her sister, Kristine; fifty years later Betsy is still hustling and bustling behind the counter seven days a week. Betsy grew up on the Menemsha docks, running around barefoot with her friends at night. "It wouldn't be a night out without a splinter or stubbed toe every once in a while!" she laughs. She hated scallops as a kid ("too sweet!") but loves them now, especially candy-like bays, seared quickly in a hot pan. But nothing beats her favorite: stuffed lobster. Her eyes light up when she shares the recipe. "This isn't an everyday dish. Save it for Valentine's Day or birthdays." Be generous with the stuffing, just as Betsy likes it. And if you don't want to split the lobsters, ask your fishmonger to help. "Have a relationship with the people you source your food from," she advises. "Speak to your fishmonger. And speak to your butcher. I learn from my customers as much as they learn from me."

SERVES 4

4 (1¼-pound) live lobsters

8 tablespoons (1 stick) unsalted butter

2½ sleeves Ritz crackers, crushed but not pulverized

2 tablespoons Italian seasoning

1 tablespoon fresh lemon juice

Sweet paprika

Lemon wedges and melted butter for serving

Split the lobsters in half or have your fishmonger split them for you. Remove the tomalley (green-yellow liver) and reserve, if desired.

Preheat the oven to 400°F. Melt the butter in a medium saucepan over low heat. Off the heat, add the crushed crackers and mix with a silicone spatula to coat the crumbs in the butter, then mix in the Italian seasoning and lemon juice. Gently fold in the tomalley, if desired. If the mixture seems overly dry, add a little extra melted butter or water.

Place the lobsters on a baking tray. Pack the mixture into the lobster bodies and onto the tails. Sprinkle each with paprika. Bake for 15 minutes, then broil for 2 minutes for a golden brown finish. Serve immediately with lemon wedges and melted butter.

Tequila-Lime Shrimp Tacos
with Pineapple Salsa & Crema

FISH MV, VINEYARD HAVEN

New England raw bar meets West Coast vibes. Sitting on the patio in the summertime with a cool cocktail, you might feel like you're in Venice Beach instead of Vineyard Haven, if not for the catboats on the Sound and the locally sourced oysters and clams shucked to order. These vibrant tacos are packed with feisty flavors. Tequila! Lime! The marinade, made the day before, guarantees juicy, bouncy shrimp that also taste great over a bowl of steamed jasmine rice with black beans and avocado.

MAKES 8 TACOS; SERVES 4

Shrimp

1 pound large shrimp, peeled and deveined

3 to 4 tablespoons olive oil

2 tablespoons tequila

1 tablespoon cilantro leaves

2 cloves garlic, crushed

1½ teaspoons honey

½ teaspoon smoked paprika

½ teaspoon kosher salt

½ teaspoon freshly ground black pepper

Finely grated zest and juice of 1 lime

Crema

1 cup full-fat sour cream

2 teaspoons cilantro leaves

Finely grated zest and juice of ½ lime

Pinch ground cumin

1 clove garlic, minced

Kosher salt and freshly ground black pepper

Salsa

Vegetable oil for grate

½ pineapple, peeled, cored, and cut into ½-inch-thick wedges

⅔ cup diced tomato

¼ cup diced red bell pepper

¼ cup minced cilantro

½ small jalapeño, seeded and minced

2 teaspoons extra virgin olive oil

Finely grated zest and juice of ½ lime

½ teaspoon kosher salt

½ teaspoon freshly ground black pepper

Assembly

8 corn tortillas

½ cup shredded napa cabbage

Microgreens for garnish

2 limes, quartered

Make the shrimp: In a large bowl, combine the shrimp, 2 tablespoons olive oil, tequila, cilantro, garlic, honey, paprika, salt, pepper, and lime zest and juice. Cover and refrigerate for 24 hours.

Make the crema: In a small bowl, combine the sour cream, cilantro, lime zest and juice, cumin, and garlic. Season with salt and pepper.

Make the salsa: Just before serving, preheat a grill to medium heat and lightly oil the grate with vegetable oil. Grill the pineapple until caramelized, about 3 minutes per side. Remove from the grill, and when cool enough to handle, chop into ½-inch pieces. Transfer to a medium bowl and add the tomato, bell pepper, cilantro, jalapeño, olive oil, lime zest and juice, salt, and pepper. Stir to combine.

Warm tortillas on the grill or over an open flame for 10 seconds on each side. Keep warm wrapped in a kitchen towel.

Heat 1 tablespoon olive oil in a large, heavy-bottomed skillet over medium-high heat. Cook the shrimp in a single layer, in batches if necessary, for 1 to 2 minutes on each side; they should be just cooked and bright orange. Transfer the shrimp from the pan to a plate and cook the remaining shrimp, adding 1 more tablespoon of olive oil, if necessary.

Assemble the tacos: Divide the cabbage and shrimp among the tortillas, and top with some of the salsa and a spoonful of crema. Garnish each taco with microgreens and a wedge of lime.

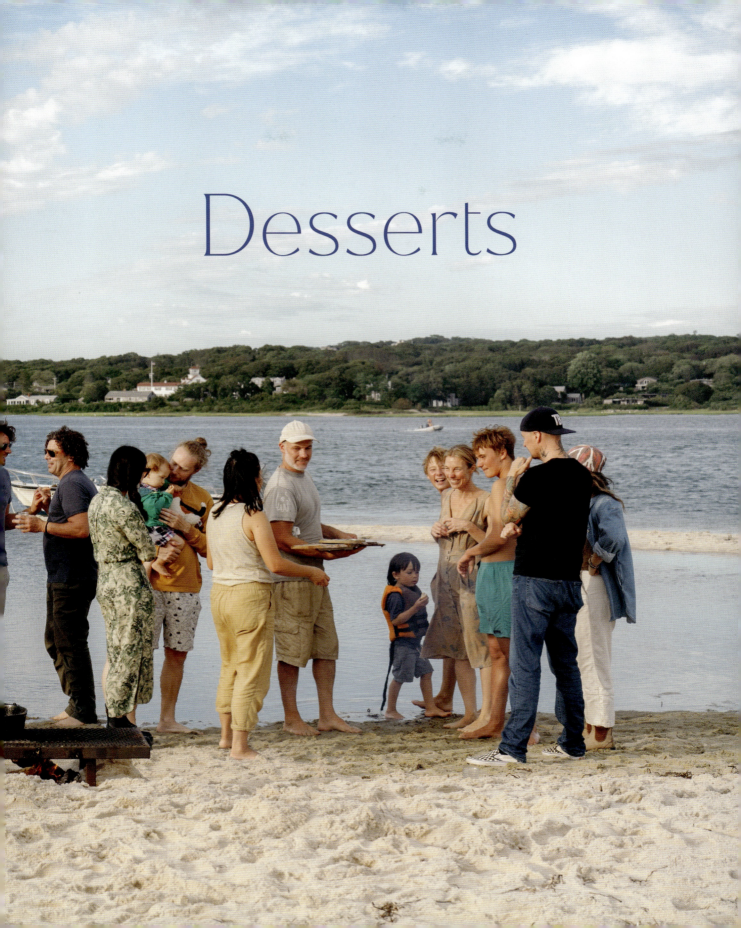

Desserts

Almond Butter Crunch

ENCHANTED CHOCOLATES, OAK BLUFFS

This is the holiday gift that became an island bestseller. Enchanted Chocolates owner Kathleen Cowley has been making almond butter crunch for over forty years, first as a gift for friends, then selling it at her family's candy store in Oak Bluffs and at the farmers market, layering hard almond toffee with dark chocolate and crushed roasted almonds. On any given day, customers drop in to buy boxes of butter crunch and fudge—or its brown sugar cousin, penuche—often reminiscing about their childhood summers on the Vineyard, then adding a box of taffy out of pure nostalgia.

MAKES 8 CUPS

4 cups slivered almonds

4 sticks (1 pound) unsalted butter, diced, plus more for pan

2 cups sugar

1 teaspoon vanilla extract

1 cup dark chocolate wafers

Preheat the oven to 325°F. Spread the almonds on a large baking sheet and roast until light golden, about 5 minutes. Cool slightly, then pulse in a food processor fitted with the metal blade into a mix of fine and coarse pieces. Lightly butter the same baking sheet.

Combine the 4 sticks butter, sugar, and ½ cup water in a medium saucepan over medium heat. Cook, stirring frequently, until the mixture is golden brown or an instant-read thermometer reads 300°F, 12 to 15 minutes. (The mixture will bubble and stay pale for most of that time, then turn brown; watch carefully as it can burn quickly at this point.) To test, spoon a drop of caramel into a glass of ice water. If it hardens and is brittle enough to break with your fingers, it's ready.

Remove from the heat and stir in half the almonds. Add the vanilla and stir again. Pour onto the prepared baking sheet and spread with an offset spatula. Let it set until hard, about 10 minutes, then turn it over.

Melt the chocolate wafers in a small saucepan over low heat or in a microwave-safe bowl in 20-second increments, stirring and repeating until smooth. Spread half of the chocolate over the butter crunch, then sprinkle with half of the remaining almonds. Refrigerate for 10 minutes.

Remove and loosen the butter crunch with an offset spatula. Turn the butter crunch over. If the chocolate has grown too stiff to pour, gently reheat it. Spread the remaining melted chocolate on the other side of the butter crunch. Sprinkle with the remaining almonds. Refrigerate until set, about 1 hour. Break apart with your hands into your preferred size. Eat immediately or store in an airtight container for up to 1 week at room temperature.

Banana Ferry Sundae

This is less a recipe and more of a forget-me-not to Vineyard summers. Mad Martha's has been serving up scoops with a side of whimsy since 1971. In true island spirit, the ice cream shop partners with other island institutions to create some of its top sellers—salted caramel with MV Sea Salt and a perky coffee with Chilmark Coffee Company (which makes a fantastic affogato, see page 241). But it's hard to beat the simple pleasure of a banana split, even as a big kid. Go on, get messy.

SERVES 1 (OR 2, IF YOU HAVE TO SHARE)

1 banana, halved lengthwise	Hot chocolate fudge sauce (see Tip)
3 scoops of your favorite ice cream	Maraschino cherries
Whipped cream	Sprinkles

In a bowl, layer the banana, followed by the ice cream, clouds of whipped cream, rivers of fudge, and cherries on top. Make it rain sprinkles with sheer abandon.

Tip: For a quick 2-ingredient chocolate fudge sauce: Place 1 (14-ounce) can sweetened condensed milk and 1½ cups semisweet or dark chocolate chips in a microwave-safe bowl. Microwave for 1 minute, stir, then microwave for 1 additional minute. Stir until smooth. Store leftovers in an airtight container in the refrigerator.

Brazilian Flan

VINEYARD GROCER, VINEYARD HAVEN

Elio Silva was working in Boston in the late 1980s when some friends of his wanted to visit Martha's Vineyard to look for work. He drove them down, and his two-week vacation turned into two weeks' notice. Growing up in a rural farming town with only nine hundred people in Brazil, the Vineyard, where everyone knows one another, felt like home.

Vineyard Grocer, Elio's red barn stocked with international ingredients and homemade prepared foods, is a mainstay for all, not only for the Brazilian community. "We have people from every culture here on the Vineyard," says Elio, "and they all tell me it feels like home when they walk through the door." He grows much of the produce they use and sell on his regenerative farm in West Bridgewater, Massachusetts. This means there are no days off, and Elio is up at three a.m. working twenty-hour days. "You know what they say: If you love what you do, you'll never work a day in your life," he says.

There's an air of conviviality at Vineyard Grocer as customers fill their baskets with linguiça, bacalhau, and plantains and grab coxinho (fried croquettes) for a snack. "Everyone is homesick, so we make food from all regions," Elio shares. One recipe that crosses borders is flan, a must for holidays and special occasions. Made with only five ingredients, it's silky smooth and luscious, with a pool of caramel syrup.

"I have customers who came to the store twenty years ago with their moms, and who now bring their kids," says Elio, smiling. "I hope one day these kids will bring their kids, too."

SERVES 6

3 large eggs

1 (14-ounce) can sweetened condensed milk

1¾ cups whole milk

1¾ cups heavy cream

¾ cup sugar

Mixed berries for serving

Position a rack in the lower third of the oven and preheat the oven to 350°F. Place a 9-inch flan ring pan or tube pan in a deep roasting pan.

With a blender, blend the eggs until smooth. Add the condensed milk, whole milk, and cream and blend again. Strain the mixture through a fine-mesh sieve into a large measuring cup (straining removes any lumps and ensures a silky-smooth custard).

Combine the sugar and ⅓ cup water in a small saucepan over medium heat. Bring to a simmer, then continue simmering until the mixture turns deep amber, about 13 minutes. It will bubble and stay pale for most of that time; do not stir, and watch carefully as the caramel can burn quickly. Immediately pour it into the flan pan.

Stir the custard and gently pour it over the caramel. Cover the pan tightly with foil. Pour boiling water into the roasting pan to reach halfway up the side of the flan pan. Bake until the flan is lightly set with a slight jiggle in the center, about 45 minutes.

Cool the flan in the roasting pan at room temperature for 1 hour. Loosen the flan from the sides of the pan by running a paring knife around the inside and outside rims. Place plastic wrap over the flan and refrigerate for at least 4 hours or overnight. Remove plastic wrap. Place a large serving plate on top of the pan, and, holding both plate and pan tightly, quickly flip to invert. Lift off the pan. The flan should slide out. If the flan sticks, dip the base of the pan in a bowl of warm water for 1 to 2 minutes to loosen the caramel and try again. Scatter berries around the flan and serve.

Brigadeiros

These Brazilian bonbons are addictive. Made with only four ingredients (plus sprinkles!), they are more than the sum of their parts. These fudgy, chocolatey bites are popular at parties, but really, who can resist them at any time of day, pretty as they are in their mini cupcake liners? As an alternative to the sprinkles, you can roll the chocolate balls in chopped pistachios or toasted coconut flakes.

MAKES 20 TO 25 BRIGADEIROS

2 tablespoons unsalted butter, plus more for pan and hands

1 (14-ounce) can sweetened condensed milk

3 tablespoons unsweetened cocoa powder

Pinch kosher salt

½ cup chocolate sprinkles

Lightly butter a large baking sheet. Melt the 2 tablespoons butter in a small saucepan over low heat, then add the condensed milk, cocoa powder, and salt. Whisk until fully combined.

Increase the heat to medium. Continue cooking, stirring constantly with a silicone spatula, until the mixture becomes very thick and shiny and the spatula leaves a clean line when scraped across the bottom, 10 to 12 minutes. (Don't be tempted to turn up the heat or stop stirring; the mixture can burn or form lumps.)

Transfer the mixture to the buttered baking sheet. Refrigerate, uncovered, until cold and firm, about 1 hour.

Place the sprinkles on a plate. With lightly buttered hands, pinch off small pieces of the chocolate mixture and roll into 1-inch balls. Roll in the sprinkles. Place in mini cupcake liners. Repeat with the remaining chocolate. Refrigerate brigadeiros in an airtight container until serving and for up to 2 weeks. Serve them cold or at room temperature.

Choose-It-Your-Way Fruit Pie

PIE CHICKS, VINEYARD HAVEN

Chrissy Kinsman knows a thing or two about pies. She's been baking them from the wee age of six, rolling out dough alongside her mother with her Grandma Helen's rolling pin—the same rolling pin she uses to this day. Every Saturday and Wednesday morning at the farmers market, fans line up to bring home one of her freshly made pies, generously filled with the season's most delicious fruit. Blueberry and key lime are summer's bestsellers, and then pumpkin, Chrissy's favorite, takes over in the fall. Back in the kitchen of her Vineyard Haven bakery, her "pie chicks" radiate a togetherness rarely seen behind the scenes, testament to the kinship Chrissy has cultivated.

Lest you be intimidated at the thought of making your own pie, Chrissy believes anyone can turn out a pie as glorious as hers by respecting the technique and putting your heart into it. "You can definitely taste the love we bake into each and every pie," shares Chrissy. "A pie baked without love, well, it's just a waste of everyone's time!" Use any high-pectin fruit—apples, pears, berries, and stone fruit, or a combination, like their popular peach and blueberry—then follow Chrissy's tips to ensure your pie is as tender and flaky as grandma's:

- Be gentle with the dough! Overhandling makes the piecrust tough.

- Cold butter and cold water equal light, flaky, melt-in-the-mouth dough.

- If your dough is hard to roll out, let it rest for 10 minutes at room temperature (but not much longer in the heat of summer).

- Get ahead of entertaining by freezing the dough discs for up to 1 month. To thaw, place in the refrigerator overnight.

MAKES ONE (9-INCH) PIE; SERVES 6 TO 8

Crust

2 cups all-purpose flour, plus more for rolling

1½ teaspoons granulated sugar

1 teaspoon kosher salt

1 stick (8 tablespoons) cold unsalted butter (preferably European-style, such as Plugra), cut into ½-inch cubes

¼ cup plus 1 tablespoon shortening

2 tablespoons whole milk

2 tablespoons turbinado sugar

Filling

5 cups fruit, such as blueberries and large chunks pitted peaches

¾ cup granulated sugar

¼ cup plus 1 tablespoon all-purpose flour

½ teaspoon fresh lemon juice and/or ½ teaspoon finely grated lemon zest

Make the pie crust: Whisk the 2 cups flour, granulated sugar, and salt in a large bowl to combine. Use your fingers to rub the butter into the flour mixture until the mixture resembles coarse, pea-size breadcrumbs. Rub the shortening into the mixture until just combined. (Alternatively, pulse the flour, sugar, and salt in the bowl of a food processor fitted with the metal blade, then pulse the butter 6 to 7 times until the mixture resembles coarse breadcrumbs. Pulse the shortening into the mixture just until combined. Transfer to a large bowl.)

Sprinkle ¼ cup ice water over the mixture and gently incorporate with a silicone spatula until the dough just holds together. If it's still dry, mix in ice water, 1 tablespoon at a time, until the dough comes together.

Divide the dough into 2 equal pieces. Shape each half into a ball, then flatten into a disk. Wrap each disk tightly with plastic wrap and refrigerate for at least 1 hour and up to 24 hours.

Lightly flour a large piece of parchment paper. Unwrap the first disc of dough and place on the parchment paper. Lightly flour the disc and cover with another piece of parchment paper. Using a rolling pin, roll the disc from the center outward, turning and lightly re-flouring the disc to make sure the dough does not stick. Roll as thin as possible without tearing the dough. If the dough is hard to roll out, let it rest for a few minutes and try again.

Remove the parchment paper and press the dough into a 9-inch pie dish. Trim the overhang so that it extends ½ inch over the edge. Roll out the second dough disc as described previously. This will be the top crust. Place on a plate lined with parchment paper and refrigerate, along with the pie dish with the dough, until ready to assemble.

Position a rack in the center of the oven and preheat the oven to 375°F.

Make the filling: Mix the fruit, sugar, flour, and lemon juice and/or zest in a large bowl until combined. Remove the dough from the refrigerator and scoop the fruit filling into the pie dish. Place the top piece of dough over the pie dish. Fold or tuck the edges of the dough together. With fingers or a fork, crimp the edges to seal. Cut several slits in the top crust to allow steam to escape. Lightly brush the top of the pie with the milk and sprinkle with turbinado sugar. Place the pie dish on a baking sheet to catch drips.

Bake until the top is golden brown and the filling bubbles up through the slits in the crust, about 50 minutes. Cool on a rack for 1 hour and serve slightly warm or at room temperature.

Fig & Honey Tart

ORANGE PEEL BAKERY, AQUINNAH

Beekeeping is mysterious magic to most of us. We mere mortals find it bewitching to watch bees collect nectar, buzzing among the wildflowers. For multi-hyphenates like Juli Vanderhoop, beekeeping is an immersion, in her case one that has captivated her for over fifteen years. Now a master beekeeper, Juli produces the delicious raw Black Brook honey, which changes nuance in flavor and color throughout the seasons. And then there are the health benefits. "Don't overheat honey, or it will kill off the beneficial antioxidants," advises Juli. "Instead of baking with honey, drizzle it over the dish, like with this tart." This recipe is a lesson in flexibility. "Use what you have," encourages Juli. If figs aren't available, sub with stone fruit, and mix in peach or pear jam instead of fig. "I'd eat this for breakfast!" says Juli laughing, and you should, too.

MAKES ONE (8-INCH) TART

5 ounces goat cheese

½ cup mascarpone

1½ teaspoons thyme leaves

½ teaspoon kosher salt

¼ cup fig jam

All-purpose flour, for dusting

1 sheet frozen all-butter puff pastry, thawed according to package instructions

4 figs, quartered

Local honey for drizzling

Preheat the oven to 400°F. Beat the goat cheese and mascarpone in a small bowl with a wooden spoon until fluffy. Fold in 1 teaspoon of the thyme and the salt, then fold in the fig jam until incorporated.

Lightly flour your work surface and roll out the pastry so it is about ¼ inch thick. Cut a 9-inch circle to fit an 8-inch tart pan with removable base with ½-inch crust up the sides. Prick the pastry all over with a fork. Fit the pastry into the pan and gently press the crust into the sides. Line with parchment paper and fill with pie weights or sugar. Blind bake for 12 minutes. Remove the parchment paper and weights, then cool completely. Leave the oven on.

Spread the goat cheese–jam mixture over the base, leaving a ½-inch border, and arrange the fig quarters on top. Bake until the cheese is light brown in spots, 18 to 20 minutes. Sprinkle with the remaining thyme and a drizzle of honey.

Honey Brûléed Brie

ISLAND BEE COMPANY, VINEYARD HAVEN

Honey is a reflection of place, as Tricia and Tim Colon's nectar shows. Their honey is raw and single-sourced from the island's six towns. Each has its own distinctive flavor profile. Chilmark, for example, is light in hue and delicate; Edgartown is molasses-deep, rich, and treacly. It's a full-time job producing up to three thousand pounds of honey every year, with climate change—especially drought—creating new challenges every season. But Tricia says their customers make it all worth it: "They value how much hard work goes into it, and come back year after year." One customer buys a case of honey for her dogs' well-being. Others eat it by the spoonful. Tricia loves it drizzled over Mermaid Farm yogurt, mixed into salad dressing, and in this minimum-effort, maximum-reward dessert (or appetizer). It might just be the easiest recipe in the book, which means you should make it this weekend and enjoy with a glass of bubbles.

SERVES 6

1 (8-ounce) round brie

1 tablespoon raw honey, such as Island Bee Company, plus more for drizzling

1 tablespoon turbinado sugar

Toasts for serving

Preheat the oven to 350°F. Place the brie on a small baking sheet. Slice the white layer of rind off the top. (If the brie came in a wooden container, place it back inside, cut side up, and return to the baking sheet.)

Spread the honey over the top of the cheese. Sprinkle the sugar in an even layer over the honey. Bake until the sugar melts, 4 to 5 minutes. Preheat the broiler. Broil until the sugar has caramelized in spots, 2 to 3 minutes. Watch carefully so it doesn't burn.

Allow to rest at room temperature until the sugar hardens, 2 to 3 minutes. Serve with toasts.

Island Flower Tartlets
with Morning Glory Strawberries

There are hidden treasures all over this island. Behind the Bookstore is a respite off humming Main Street, tucked away behind Edgartown Books (support local bookstores!). Come for the stellar coffee and stay for the baked goods, crafted by Deva Randolph and Jessica Noe. "We bake what we crave," says Deva of their inspirations, like these pretty tartlets topped with Morning Glory Farm strawberries, which taste like summer in every bite.

MAKES EIGHT (4-INCH) TARTLETS

Pie Dough

1 stick plus
5 tablespoons (180 g)
cold unsalted butter

1½ cups (200 g)
all-purpose flour

⅓ cup (50 g) kamut
or spelt flour

1 teaspoon (4 g) sugar

½ teaspoon (4 g)
kosher salt

½ teaspoon distilled
white vinegar

Flower Pastry Cream

2¼ cups (500 g)
whole milk

4 ounces (113 g)
edible flowers

8 large egg yolks (120 g)

½ cup plus
2 tablespoons
(122 g) sugar

¼ cup plus
2 tablespoons
(50 g) cornstarch

5 tablespoons
(75 g) unsalted
butter, cubed and at
room temperature

Almond Cream and Finishing

1¾ cups (180 g)
almond flour

1 stick plus
3 tablespoons
(150 g) unsalted
butter, softened

1⅓ cups (150 g)
confectioners' sugar,
plus ¼ cup (25 g)
for finishing

¾ teaspoon (6 g)
kosher salt

1 tablespoon plus
1 teaspoon (15 g)
almond extract

1 tablespoon (8 g)
all-purpose flour

20 medium
strawberries

Edible flowers
for finishing

Make the pie dough: Grate the butter on the large holes of a box grater. Place on a baking sheet and freeze until solid, about 30 minutes. In a large bowl, combine the flours, sugar, and salt. Combine the vinegar with ½ cup ice water. Toss the frozen butter into the bowl with the flour mixture. Break up any big clumps of butter by hand. Make a well in the center of the bowl and add ¼ cup of the water and vinegar mixture while folding in the ingredients with a spatula. Continue adding liquid about 1 tablespoon at a time just until the dough holds together when pressed with your hands. You may not need the full amount.

Turn the dough onto a work surface and press into a small disk. Halve the dough and place one half on top of the other. Press together to create one piece. Wrap tightly in plastic wrap and refrigerate for at least 1 hour and up to 24 hours.

Make the flower pastry cream: Place the milk and flowers in a medium saucepan and scald over medium heat (until small bubbles appear around the edge). Do not boil. Remove from the heat and place a piece of parchment paper directly on the milk so it does not form a skin; let sit at room temperature for at least 30 minutes and up to 1 hour.

In a large bowl, whisk together the egg yolks, sugar, and cornstarch.

Strain the milk into a large measuring cup and discard the flowers. Return the infused milk to the saucepan and scald over medium-high heat. Add the hot milk in a thin stream to the egg yolk mixture, whisking constantly. Pour the mixture back into the saucepan and stir constantly over medium heat until bubbles appear, about 5 minutes. Remove from the heat and add the cubed butter a few pieces at a time, whisking between additions until fully incorporated.

Line a baking sheet with parchment paper. Force the pastry cream through a strainer or chinois onto the prepared pan to remove any lumps. Place plastic wrap directly on the surface of the pastry cream and refrigerate until cool, about 1 hour.

Make the almond cream: Preheat the oven to 350°F. Spread the almond flour on a small baking sheet and toast until it smells nutty, 5 to 10 minutes. Remove and cool completely.

In a stand mixer fitted with the paddle attachment, cream the butter on high speed until smooth, about 1 minute. Add the confectioners' sugar, toasted almond flour, and salt and mix on medium speed until combined, about 1 minute. Add the almond extract and all-purpose flour and continue mixing on medium speed, about 1 additional minute. Cover and refrigerate for 1 hour.

To assemble, roll out the dough to ⅛ inch thick and cut out eight 6-inch circles.

Line eight 4-inch tart pans with removable bases with the dough. Trim excess dough as the pan will not release from the crust if there is dough hanging over the edge. Place the lined pans in the freezer until the dough is frozen, about 1 hour.

Preheat the oven to 350°F. Remove the pans from the freezer and place on a large baking sheet. Line each

crust with parchment paper and fill with pie weights or sugar (which you can reuse). Bake until the surface of the dough is dry and light golden, 12 to 15 minutes. Remove the parchment paper and pie weights and bake until the dough is fully cooked, 12 to 15 additional minutes. Remove the crusts but leave the oven on.

Cool the crusts for 15 minutes. Divide the almond cream among the tarts and spread with an offset spatula. Return to the oven and bake until the almond cream is a light golden color, about 12 minutes. Cool to room temperature.

Unmold the tarts. Transfer the pastry cream to a piping bag and pipe the cream into each tart up to the top of the crust. Thinly slice the strawberries crosswise and layer them on top of the pastry cream. Lightly dust the tarts with the remaining confectioners' sugar for extra shine. Finish with edible flowers.

Key Lime Bars

KORILEE CONNELLY, OAK BLUFFS

Is there a dreamier team than the Mo's Lunch crew and dessert queen Korilee Connelly? It's impossible to pick up a sandwich or dinner plate at Mo's without indulging in one of Korilee's sweet treats. The island-born baker rises early to whip up whimsical takes on doughnuts, cookies, and cakes—think ice-cream sundae cupcakes or these popular key lime bars. Korilee doesn't play by the rules, so instead of your typical graham cracker crust, rich and buttery shortbread stands in as the base for the luscious lime topping, making them a cross between cheesecake and pie (because two desserts are better than one, right?). Korilee often uses regular limes for their availability, so use what you have.

MAKES 12 BARS

Crust

2 sticks (½ pound) unsalted butter, melted

½ cup sugar

3¼ cups all-purpose flour, plus more if needed

Butter for pan

Filling

1 (14-ounce) can sweetened condensed milk

¾ cup full-fat sour cream

6 tablespoons fresh key lime or lime juice (from about 9 key limes or 3 large limes)

Finely grated zest of 1 large lime, plus more for finishing

Make the crust: Preheat the oven to 350°F. Combine the melted butter and sugar in a large bowl, then add the flour in two additions, mixing well to combine between additions. The dough should clump together when pressed with your fingers. If it's humid and the mix is too soft to clump, add more flour about 1 tablespoon at a time to achieve the right consistency.

Butter a 9 by 13–inch pan and line with parchment paper, letting the short ends hang over the sides (you'll use it as a sling to lift out the bars). Transfer the dough to the pan and press it evenly with your fingers. Bake until lightly golden, 17 to 20 minutes. Remove from the oven and cool. Keep the oven on.

Make the filling: Whisk the condensed milk and sour cream in a medium bowl until completely smooth. Add the lime juice and zest and mix again. Pour the mixture over the cooled crust and bake until set, 8 to 12 minutes. Sprinkle additional lime zest on top. Cool completely in the pan on a rack. Refrigerate until ready to serve, then lift out in one piece using the parchment paper overhang. With a sharp knife, slice into 12 bars just before serving.

Salted Caramel Pots de Crème

MV SEA SALT, VINEYARD HAVEN

Heidi Feldman and Curtis Friedman's sea change could be the inspiration for a summer beach bestseller. Unbeknownst to them, the couple grew up ten minutes from each other in Connecticut; they met in Boston in their early twenties. After vacationing on the Vineyard for a decade, it was time to make the move, and in 2001, that's exactly what they did. Two years later, they founded Down Island Farm, juggling farming with their day jobs. When disease devastated the farm, the dynamic duo got to brainstorming, and wouldn't you know, an idea came to them over lunch and a pack of Cape Cod salt and vinegar chips. Sea salt! When Heidi could not find a locally produced salt, on an island surrounded by crystal clear salt water, it was the ah-ha moment they were looking for.

Their vision was also crystal clear: Produce the finest sea salt using nothing but sustainable solar energy, salt water, and sunshine. And, of course, plenty of elbow grease. But even on a bitingly crisp January morning collecting salt water off the beach (thanks to a state license that took months to procure), Heidi is beaming. "I love what we do!" Their raw sea salt is treated gently, not heated beyond 115°F, and never touched by carbon fuels. It can take anywhere from three to twelve weeks to dry depending on the temperature, weather conditions, and angle of the sun. "We opt for a slower but eco-friendly solar drying process," says Heidi, "because our customers and the planet deserve nothing but the best."

In 2013, MV Sea Salt was born, with flavors that pay homage to the region, such as blueberry honey and smoked oak (try it on grilled veg). It doesn't get much more local than this dessert from pastry chef Marnely Murray made with island milk, honey, and, of course, sea salt. It's deceptively simple yet impressive, and can be made ahead, a gift to entertainers and potluckers.

MAKES SIX (6- TO 8-OUNCE) RAMEKINS

Custards

1 cup heavy cream

1 cup whole milk

⅔ cup local honey, such as Island Bee Company

¼ teaspoon sea salt, such as MV Sea Salt, plus more for finishing

2 large eggs

1 egg yolk

1 teaspoon vanilla extract

Salted Caramel Sauce

½ cup sugar

½ cup local honey

1 cup heavy cream

1 teaspoon vanilla extract

1½ teaspoons sea salt

Make the custards: Preheat the oven to 325°F. Place six 6- to 8-ounce ramekins in a baking dish.

Simmer the heavy cream, milk, honey, and ¼ teaspoon sea salt in a medium saucepan over medium-low heat. Whisk the eggs, yolk, and vanilla in a large bowl. Once the cream mixture comes to a simmer, add it to the egg mixture in a thin stream, whisking constantly.

Strain the mixture through a sieve into a large measuring cup. (Don't skip this step! Straining ensures a smooth custard.) Pour evenly among the ramekins. Cover each ramekin tightly with foil. Fill the baking dish halfway up the sides of the ramekins with boiling water.

Bake the custards for 30 minutes. They should jiggle slightly in the center. If the custards are too loose, return them to the oven and check every 5 minutes. The custards will continue to cook once they're removed from the oven. Allow the custards to cool completely in the pan, then remove the ramekins and refrigerate for at least 2 hours, and preferably overnight.

Make the sauce: Combine the sugar, honey, and ¼ cup water in a deep, medium stainless steel pot. Brush the sides of the pan with a wet brush. Turn the heat to high, and cook until golden brown, about 8 minutes (every stove is different so watch for the color more than the time). Don't step away as the caramel can quickly burn. Carefully pour in the cream and whisk—the mixture will bubble up. Whisk in the vanilla and salt and cook for 2 additional minutes. Transfer to an airtight container, cover, and cool.

Spoon sauce over each pot and finish with sea salt.

Drinks

Double Coffee Syrup

Vineyarders love their coffee. And Vineyarders love Todd Christy, founder of the original island roaster, Chilmark Coffee Company. It's easy to understand why: Todd has an infectious obsession with exceptional coffee. He selects the finest beans from small farms in Colombia, Guatemala, Honduras, Brazil, Ethiopia, Rwanda, and Burundi, seeking out producers that allow farmers to earn a fair living. Then it's home to Chilmark to roast, bag, deliver, and repeat—these beans get snapped up quickly when they hit the shelves. Todd came up with this genius coffee syrup when catering summer events. Brewed twice—wait, it's hardly any extra effort!—the result is a concentrated coffee sweetened to your taste, and it's super versatile. Try it as an affogato (shown in photo), swirled into a mocha milkshake, or in an espresso martini—the ideal pick-me-up before a night on the (Edgar)town.

MAKES ½ CUP

½ cup sugar

½ cup (40 g) dark roast coffee beans (such as Chilmark Coffee Company Squibnocket)

Combine the sugar and ½ cup water in a small saucepan over medium-low heat. Cook, stirring occasionally, until sugar is dissolved, about 4 minutes. Remove this simple syrup from the heat.

For the pour-over method, boil 2 cups of water. Grind the coffee beans to a medium-fine grind. Weigh out half of the ground coffee beans. Add 1½ cups boiled water, and brew for 4 minutes. Pour the first brew over the remainder of the ground coffee beans, and brew again for 4 minutes. (Alternatively, use your favorite brewing method such as French press, AeroPress, or drip to brew the coffee twice.)

Transfer the coffee to a small saucepan and bring to a simmer over medium-low heat. Add the simple syrup 1 tablespoon at a time, stirring to combine. Begin tasting for sweetness after 3 tablespoons. Continue adding 1 tablespoon of syrup until you reach your desired sweetness, keeping in mind that as the syrup reduces the sweetness will concentrate. Simmer over low heat until slightly viscous, 30 to 40 minutes. Pour into a heatproof glass jar with a lid to cool; cool uncovered. The syrup will continue to thicken slightly as it stands. Once cool, cover and refrigerate for up to 5 days. Any leftover simple syrup can be stored in an airtight container in the refrigerator for up to 1 month.

Espresso Float

Adam Petkus, Evan Hammond, and Todd Hitchings go way back with the island's annual Agricultural Fair. Friends from kindergarten in West Tisbury, they started off at age ten as Fair trash kids who worked the recycling, compost, and trash stations. Fast forward to summer 2009, with twenty-one-year-old Adam hoping to put away a few bucks before returning to college. His father, Ken, thought a root beer float stand at the Fair might be easy enough to pull off. Along for the ride came high school buddy Mike Shea, and the colorful Floaters booth was born. "But not everyone wants a root beer float first thing in the morning," says Adam. "So we came up with the espresso float. No one says no to an affogato." They began making their now-signature floats using free coffeemakers found at the Dumptique recycling shed. At first, they used mass-produced espresso grounds, which lacked depth and clashed with their desire to source locally where possible. They quickly upgraded to a fancy espresso maker and turned their team into baristas, choosing locally roasted Chilmark Coffee Company whole espresso beans. "Nothing beats the look on the face of fairgoers after that first sip," beams Adam. Today, the Floaters booth is a collaboration of local families, all proud to offer unique Fair fare and be part of the fabric of the West Tisbury community.

MAKES 1 FLOAT

1 large scoop
vanilla ice cream

2 shots hot espresso,
preferably from
Chilmark Coffee
Company beans

1 tablespoon crumbled
amaretti cookies

Pinch ground cinnamon

Chocolate syrup
for finishing

Whipped cream
for finishing

Put the ice cream in a tumbler glass and pour the espresso over the top. Sprinkle with the amaretti and cinnamon, then drizzle with chocolate syrup and finish with a tower of whipped cream.

Golden Hour

Brett Nevin has a way with cocktails. After honing his mixology skills at Atria and at Gramercy Tavern in New York, among other places, Brett launched his private bartending service with a roving barrel bar and a tiki hut on wheels. A cocktail history buff, Brett pays homage to the classics while tapping into his arsenal of craft liquors from around the world to create his own signature sips. This tropical margarita is his homage to that magical time of day on the island—post-beach, pre-sunset—when everything glows. The recipe can easily be scaled up for a party.

MAKES 1 DRINK

2 lime wedges

Sea salt, such as MV Sea Salt's Turmeric, Cranberry & White Pepper salt, for rim

1½ ounces tequila (such as Espolon Reposado)

¾ ounce Chinola mango liqueur

¾ ounce fresh lime juice

¾ ounce pineapple-carrot juice (best-quality store-bought or freshly squeezed)

¼ ounce Cointreau

¼ ounce fruity hot sauce, such as TigerHawk's pineapple-habanero hot sauce (optional)

Pineapple leaves and carrot for garnish (optional)

Rub 1 lime wedge around the rim of a tumbler glass. Place salt on a small dish and rub the rim in the salt. Fill the glass with ice.

Pour the tequila, mango liqueur, lime juice, pineapple-carrot juice, Cointreau, and hot sauce, if using, into a cocktail shaker, fill with ice, and shake for 30 seconds. Strain into the glass and serve with the remaining lime wedge. Garnish with the pineapple leaves and carrot, if desired.

Pineapple Mint Daiquiri

NOMANS, OAK BLUFFS

Summertime and the living is easy at Nomans. It's got the food, the drinks, the lawn games, and live music. Nomans bottles its own rum, inspired by its namesake, an uninhabited island three miles off the southwest coast of Aquinnah where rum runners stashed their liquid gold during Prohibition. At Triple 8 Distillery on neighboring Nantucket, Nomans white rum is aged in new American oak barrels for three years, then bottled. Channel your inner pirate and island hop through the cocktail list, or ease into the groove with this light and refreshing pineapple mint daiquiri. Make a big batch and turn up the tunes.

MAKES 1 DRINK

Ice for shaking

2 ounces pineapple juice

1½ ounces Nomans white rum

½ ounce fresh lime juice

¼ ounce simple syrup

2 fresh mint leaves

1 small pineapple wedge

Fill a cocktail shaker with ice. Add the pineapple juice, rum, lime juice, and simple syrup. Cover and shake for 30 seconds. Strain into a martini glass. Smack the mint leaves between your hands to release the aroma and float them on top. Garnish with the pineapple wedge.

Naughty or Nice Hot Cocoa
with Salted Honey Whipped Cream

YOMMI, VINEYARD HAVEN

Kismet. It's a word you hear often on the Vineyard. It's how Caroline Harris and Ryan Gussen describe the opportunity to take over Yommi, the well-loved natural popsicle business run out of the sweetest vintage blue 1972 Boler camper, and make it their own. Caroline spent summers at her family's gingerbread cottage in Oak Bluffs, scooping ice cream at Carousel Ice Cream. She brought her partner, Ryan, out to the island and it was love at first sight. As fans of Yommi's paleta-inspired superfood bars, when they heard the business was up for sale, they knew it was meant to be. "We're so proud to be able to continue making healthy treats that bring people joy," says Caroline.

The couple make hundreds of pops daily by hand, flavored with Island Bee Company honey and pinches of MV Sea Salt. "There's nothing better than being part of the farmers market family and seeing little kids and big kids alike enjoying our pops," shares Ryan. Come winter, Ryan turns the flavors of their Peruvian Choco-Buzz bar into a decadent hot chocolate: Naughty has a kiss of heat, while Nice is dairy-free with the creaminess of coconut. The salted honey whipped cream is a revelation. Don't overwhip—you want billowy soft peaks that invite whipped cream moustaches.

Naughty Hot Cocoa
MAKES 2 MUGS

1 cup whipping cream

2 tablespoons honey, such as Island Bee Company

2 teaspoons vanilla extract

¼ teaspoon fine sea salt, such as MV Sea Salt

3 cups whole milk

3 tablespoons sweetened condensed milk

½ cup freshly brewed coffee

2 ounces 90 to 100% cacao dark chocolate, finely chopped

2 tablespoons fresh orange juice

Pinch ground cayenne pepper

Cocoa powder for dusting

Using a handheld or stand mixer fitted with a whisk attachment, whip the cream until frothy. Add the honey, 1 teaspoon vanilla, and salt. Continue whisking until soft peaks form.

Warm the milk in a small saucepan over medium-low heat until wisps of steam appear. Add the sweetened condensed milk, coffee, remaining 1 teaspoon vanilla, and chocolate. Stir over low heat until the chocolate is melted.

Add the orange juice and cayenne. Stir, then pour into 2 mugs and top with the whipped cream. Dust with cocoa powder.

Nice Hot Cocoa
MAKES 2 MUGS

1 (13½-ounce) can coconut cream, chilled overnight

⅓ cup plus 2 tablespoons honey, such as Island Bee Company

2 teaspoons vanilla extract

¼ teaspoon plus pinch fine sea salt, such as MV Sea Salt

2 (13½-ounce) cans unsweetened coconut milk

2 tablespoons unsweetened cocoa powder, plus more for dusting

2 tablespoons fresh orange juice

Pinch ground cinnamon

Scoop the solidified coconut cream into the bowl of a stand mixer fitted with the wire whisk, leaving any liquid behind. Whisk for 30 seconds. Add 2 tablespoons of the honey, ½ teaspoon vanilla, and ¼ teaspoon salt. Continue whisking until soft peaks form. (Alternatively, use a handheld mixer.)

In a saucepan, combine the coconut milk, 2 tablespoons cocoa powder, and remaining ⅓ cup honey and simmer over medium-low heat, stirring constantly, until the honey has dissolved. Whisk in the remaining 1½ teaspoons vanilla, orange juice, cinnamon, and remaining pinch salt, and warm through.

Pour into 2 mugs and top with the whipped cream. Dust with cocoa powder.

Spicy Blackberry Basil Drink

AQUILA, AQUINNAH

Depending on the time of year, the path from Gay Head Lighthouse to Moshup Beach will take you through fields of yellow wildflowers, clusters of wild pink roses, or bushes of crimson bearberries. The walk is invigorating for the body and the soul, and a thirst-quenching drink awaits at Aquila. Aquinnah is a dry town, so Del and Jennifer Araujo offer a variety of coolers, which inspired this mocktail. Jennifer loves to keep it local, using fresh basil and jalapeños from Morning Glory Farm and Black Brook honey from nearby Orange Peel Bakery. Enjoy as is, or spike with tequila or gin.

MAKES 1 DRINK

1 tablespoon plus
1 teaspoon honey,
such as Black Brook

¼ cup granulated sugar

⅓ cup fresh
blackberries

¼ cup basil leaves

3 to 4 thin slices
jalapeño

1 tablespoon
maple syrup

Ice, for shaking
and serving

¼ cup fresh lime
juice (about 2 limes)

¼ cup water or
alcohol, such as
tequila or gin

Sparkling water,
for finishing

1 lime wedge,
for garnish

Pour 1 teaspoon honey and the sugar onto separate small plates. Dip the rim of a tumbler glass into the honey, then dip into the sugar.

Set aside 1 blackberry for garnish. Muddle the remaining blackberries in a cocktail shaker with a muddler or the back of a spoon and strain through a fine-mesh strainer into a small glass, pressing down to extract as much juice as possible (you'll have about 1 tablespoon).

Set aside 1 basil leaf for garnish. Add the remaining 1 tablespoon honey, remaining basil leaves, 2 to 3 slices jalapeño (reserving 1 slice for garnish), and maple syrup to the cocktail shaker. Muddle together. Fill with ice and add the blackberry juice, lime juice, and water (or alcohol). Cover and shake for 30 seconds.

Pour the drink into the prepared glass and top with sparkling water and ice. Garnish with the reserved blackberry, jalapeño slice, basil leaf, and lime wedge and serve.

Index

Acknowledgments

To the people of Noepe, thank you for welcoming us. We are so grateful to call this island home.

Juli, thank you for the beautiful words with which you welcome readers, and for being part of this project.

Jocelyn, the stars aligned for this one. What a gift to work on this book with you! You captured our island so genuinely and beautifully, and boy did we have a blast along the way. Here's to more.

To my book team, Adriana Stimola and Katie Leaird, you made this so, so fun. Big thanks to James, Tricia, Jan, Jessica, and Natalie, at Rizzoli.

To my sister, Kathy, you are such a huge part of why I fell in love with food and cooking. Once you took me to East Ocean, that was it. I love you so much and am always counting down to our next meal together.

To Will and Marianna, I'm so proud of you.

To David, always in our hearts.

To Dani, Ruth, Jo, Steve, Ralitza, Susan, Laurie, Alisha, Lerato, Sarah, Laura, my Chase family, my work family, and my dear friends. I am the luckiest to have you in my life.

I am deeply grateful to many resources, including the Martha's Vineyard libraries, Julia Cameron, The Young Turks, and the *Everything Cookbooks*, *Everything Is Fine*, and *Every Outfit* podcasts.

Special thanks to all the contributors for your dedication to your craft, your hospitality, and your deliciousness. Cheers!

Proceeds of this book will be shared with Island Grown Initiative, Kinship Heals, and other island organizations. Find out more at marthasvineyardcookbook.com.

Author Biography

Julia Blanter is a marketing director, culinary adventurer, and passionate home cook with extensive experience across the food industry. Julia's love of food has taken her into kitchens and restaurants all around the world. Born in the colorful, multicultural landscape of Sydney, Australia, Julia has lived in New Caledonia, the Netherlands, London, Brooklyn, and most recently, her island home of Martha's Vineyard.

First published in the United States of America in 2025 by
Rizzoli International Publications, Inc.
49 West 27th Street
New York, NY 10001
www.rizzoliusa.com

Copyright © 2025 Julia Blanter

Photography by Jocelyn Filley

Publisher: Charles Miers
Associate Publisher: James Muschett
Editor: Tricia Levi
Design: Jan Derevjanik
Production Manager: Colin Hough Trapp
Managing Editor: Lynn Scrabis
Copyeditor: Natalie Danford
Proofreader: Sarah Stump

ISBN: 978-0-8478-2977-4
Library of Congress Control Number: 2024945541

Printed in China
2025 2026 2027 2028 / 10 9 8 7 6 5 4 3 2

Visit us online:
Instagram.com/RizzoliBooks
Facebook.com/RizzoliNewYork
Youtube.com/user/RizzoliNY

FSC
www.fsc.org

MIX
Paper | Supporting responsible forestry
FSC® C104723